How to be a successful entrepreneur

How to be a successful entrepreneur

Spot the opportunity, take a risk and build a brilliant business

HELGA DRUMMOND

KOGAN PAGE

London and Philadelphia

Publisher's note
Every possible effort has been made to ensure that the information contained in this book
is accurate at the time of going to press, and the publishers and author cannot accept
responsibility for any errors or omissions, however caused. No responsibility for loss or
damage occasioned to any person acting, or refraining from action, as a result of the
material in this publication can be accepted by the editor, the publisher or the author.

First published in Great Britain and the United States in 2009 by Kogan Page Limited

120 Pentonville Road   525 South 4th Street, #241
London N1 9JN   Philadelphia PA 19147
United Kingdom   USA
www.koganpage.com

© Helga Drummond, 2009

The right of Helga Drummond to be identified as the author of this work has been
asserted by her in accordance with the Copyright, Designs and Patents Act 1988.

ISBN 978 0 7494 5514 9

British Library Cataloguing-in-Publication Data

A CIP record for this book is available from the British Library.

Library of Congress Cataloging-in-Publication Data

Drummond, Helga.
   How to be a successful entrepreneur : spot the opportunity, take
the risk, and build a brilliant business / Helga Drummond.
      p. cm.
   Includes index.
   ISBN 978-0-7494-5514-9
  1. Entrepreneurship. 2. Success in business. 3. Decision making.
4. New business enterprises. I. Title.
   HB615.D78 2009
   658.1'1--dc22

                                                              2009000810

Typeset by Jean Cussons Typesetting, Diss, Norfolk
Printed and bound in India by Replika Press Pvt Ltd

In memory of William Hodge Drummond, 1923–2008

Contents

Preface and Acknowledgements

In September 2002, Professor Dominic Elliott of Liverpool University Management School asked me if I would run a course on entrepreneurship – for delivery in three weeks' time. Flattered though I was by my colleague's confidence in my creative prowess, we decided that the timescale was perhaps a little ambitious. The result was a compromise plan to write a specialist MBA elective entitled 'Decision-Making for Entrepreneurs'.

The next milestone was an invitation from David Sharp of Imperial College Press (an imprint of World Scientific Publishing) to produce a textbook based on the MBA elective. Although a textbook was not what I wanted to write, I am grateful for the suggestion, as it became the inspiration for this book.

Having finally decided what I did want to write, I was heartened by the enthusiasm of Julia Swales and her colleagues at Kogan Page for the project. It is also timely to recall a similarly prompt and positive reply from Pauline Goodwin, formerly of Kogan Page, almost 20 years earlier that set me on the road in my publishing career.

Many of the insights into ownership and what makes entrepreneurs successful derive from my neighbour Stuart Rayner. One I have acknowledged directly, but the book is infused with many more. Stuart has also inspired successive generations of MBA students in Liverpool with his lively and provocative guest appearances.

I am indebted to the owners whose stories, some funny, some sad, are interwoven into the text. Some accounts come from research conducted over the years; others reflect casual conversations; and one or two are anecdotes related to me. In all cases, names and contexts have been changed to protect owners' identities. Liverpool University Management School generously funded parts of the aforementioned research and provided a congenial atmosphere for writing. I am also grateful for support from the Economic and Social Research Council (ESRC), including support for a project undertaken jointly with my Management School colleague Julia Hodgson.

Janet Briddon corrected the final draft with unfailing patience and eagle-eyed thoroughness. Julie Reddy in the Management School helped with the intricacies of Microsoft Word.

Rear-Admiral Trevor Spires CBE took time out of a daunting schedule to respond to requests for advice – not all of them connected with the present work. Brigadier Robin Bacon helped to provide an appropriate life balance by instructing me in the mysteries of croquet.

The manuscript would have been delivered to Kogan Page one day earlier but for an appointment in Kinross on 15 September 2008. Thanks to Alexander, Theresa and Martin Drummond for making it such a memorable day and to Bianca Drummond for hosting the sequel. Donald Drummond also helped out. Gannon, William, Alexander and Dominic Drummond provided a tumultuous background, along with Emma, Laura and Kate Beale.

Introduction

That wasn't luck, I deserved it.
(Margaret Thatcher)

In 1961, something remarkable happened in the Libyan desert. Eight years earlier, in 1953, an obscure entrepreneur named Bunker Hunt applied for a drilling licence. The prospects were exciting, as geologists advised Hunt that an oilfield recently discovered in Algeria would almost certainly extend into Libya. Unfortunately for Hunt, the so-called Seven Sisters (multinational oil companies) were already drilling in the best sites. The only concession available to Hunt was so far remote from the Algerian border and offered such miserable prospects that even the customary bribe to local officials was waived.

"The story could have ended there... except for Bunker's instinct. As a gambling man, he believed that the more cards he could draw on, the better his chances would be, even if the cards were those no one else thought worth picking up."

Hunt drilled for years and found nothing. Moreover, despite their markedly better chances, the Seven Sisters did no better drilling near Algeria. Eventually, one of the 'Sisters', British Petroleum (BP), gave up and went into partnership with Hunt.

"The deal did not at first change Bunker's luck. In 1961, BP's experienced drilling teams struck out into the desert and drilled one well in Block 65. They reported that it was dry. So was the second well, and the third."

The rig superintendent was instructed by BP to stop drilling and return home. It was the final shattering blow for Hunt, who had invested all his money in the venture.

"Then, just for luck, the rig superintendent drilled another 3 metres into the sand before withdrawing the bit from the third hole, and in doing so uncovered Bunker's ace. That 3 metres was enough to pierce the cap of one of the world's largest oilfields."

UNCOVERING THE ACE

We make our decisions and our decisions make us. Being an entrepreneur is like riding a roller coaster – a combination of thrills and spills. The spills are many; in the United States, 80 per cent of new start-ups fold within two years. The statistics for the United Kingdom are similarly depressing. Yet most failures are avoidable. Bad luck is not to blame; rather, ill-judged decision making. Another concern is that many entrepreneurs who do succeed in establishing themselves in business never realize anywhere near their full potential. All decisions involving uncertainty imply risk, but there is no need to learn the hard way. This book explains how to improve the odds and make your own luck.

Both nascent and experienced entrepreneurs are my target audience. That includes social entrepreneurs – the 'movers and shakers' to whom we owe organizations such as credit unions, housing associations, the 'Fair Trade' movement and women's cooperatives including the aptly named plumbing firm Stop-Cocks.

Emphatically my purpose is not to explain the mechanics of ownership, such as how to write business plans. There are many good books on those subjects and I doubt if I could improve upon them. My aim is to complement those self-help works by addressing crucial decisions:

- ∎ How do I recognize a good opportunity?
- ∎ How do I recognize a decision I might subsequently regret?
- ∎ How can I predict how a decision might turn out?
- ∎ When should I trust my instincts?
- ∎ How can I prepare for the unexpected?
- ∎ When should I take a risk?

- How should I choose if faced with two equally attractive options?
- When should I cut my losses?
- When is the best time to sell a thriving business?
- How do I get what I want and what do I need to make a success of the business?

Read on. Every time you turn a page you may be uncovering *your* ace.

NOTE

1. Fay, S (1982) *Beyond Greed*, New York, Viking, p 1–2

1

Entrepreneurial Genius

– deciding on an idea for business

Discovery consists of seeing what everybody else has seen and thinking what nobody else has thought.

(Albert von Szent-Györgyi)

Key message: Genius is a trick of mind

Tea bags, liquid soap, highlighter pens – the world is full of good, commercially viable ideas that seem obvious now but did not exist until someone thought of them. How did they do it?

Deciding on an idea for business can be difficult. The world is a crowded marketplace. There are two ways of generating new ideas. One is to wait for inspiration to strike. It may work but it is uncertain. This chapter explains how to coax ideas by applying a little DIY genius.

Emphatically, entrepreneurial genius does not require sophisticated scientific or technical knowledge. Genius resides in how we think about things. The BlackBerry mobile phone has captured a market lead in e-mail that rivals have struggled to beat. The device is packed full of complicated electronics but its success rests as much as anything on a shift in thinking. Hitherto, handheld e-mail devices had relied upon the concept of 'pull', requiring users to expend time in opening up their e-mails. In contrast, the attraction of the BlackBerry is that it is based on the opposite concept of 'pushing' e-mails out to recipients.

Clever research and development scientists worked hard to make 'pull' e-mail devices better, faster, more user-friendly and so forth. Yet so long as their thinking was constrained within the parameters of the 'pull' concept, they were limited in what they could achieve.

Genius is a trick of mind that can be learned. The trick resides in questioning the obvious, in questioning received ways of doing things and demolishing concepts that are blocking progress. Incidentally, even if you already have an idea for business or are already in business, you may still find what follows useful.

BECOMING A GENIUS

Blocking assumptions are everywhere. They frequently reside in 'taken-for-granted' assumptions and practices. For example, when we say 'pen', we almost invariably think 'ink'. It is obvious, is it not? The trouble is, if we never looked beyond the obvious, we would never have invented the electronic pen we use to sign for parcel deliveries. The aeroplane is modelled on the concept of a bird. It has wings. We can improve the wings by streamlining, but in order to invent the helicopter we needed to demolish the assumption that flying machines need wings. Shoes may have laces, but that doesn't mean that they need them. Early train carriages had compartments because they were based on the concept of horse and carriage. Open-plan seating made carriages cheaper to haul because they were lighter and accommodated more passengers, but they were only invented by dropping the original concept.

We sometimes make assumptions without realizing it. Before Allen Lane, books were expensive partly because they had cardboard covers. Lane made business history (and a fortune) by reinventing the 'book' as a paperback. Wind farms are unpopular. Critics argue that the amount of electricity generated does not justify their unsightly appearance in the rural landscape. There seems to be no easy answer — if we assume that windmills need to stand on land, that is. In fact, trials are afoot to float them at sea. Early computers occupied whole rooms. Initial efforts to make them small focused upon shrinking the hardware. The result was an incremental improvement in the shape of a slightly smaller computer. It was only when developers (including Bill Gates) stepped back from the problem and realized that if the software took up less room, computers would automatically shrink — hence the advent of the desktop PC.

It is not what is, but what might be.

What is a mobile phone these days? It might be a camera, or an MP3 player, or an organizer. It may also send and receive telephone calls and text messages. Once we drop the original concept of 'telephone' and redefine it, say, as a miniature computer, we can glimpse other possibilities.

It is a question that is exercising the banking industry because technological innovations will soon enable us to operate a bank account from a mobile phone. Once the technology is in place, there may be little to stop mobile phone companies from offering banking services.

CONCEPTUAL BLOCKBUSTING

How we conceptualize something determines *what* we see and *how* we see. If I say the word 'time', you will probably immediately think 'clock'. Yet a clock is just a human invention to help us understand the notion of 'time'. Without clocks to regulate time, life as we know it would break down. Trains could not run 'on time' (not that they do anyway); the conference call could not take place at 8 o'clock in the morning if we did not all measure time in the same way. Yet useful though the concept is, it also constrains our thinking. We think of time as something that passes, but where does it go to after it passes? We think of the past as irretrievable, yet some things happen time and time again.

More importantly, the clock moves forwards. Stephen Hawking's genius lay in realizing that physicists had unconsciously restricted their thinking by always imagining time as moving forwards. Hawking did something simple but profound. He imagined time as moving backwards as well as forwards. This insight enabled physicists to conceptualize the notion of stars collapsing backwards as they were sucked into black holes.

Possibilities are limited only by imagination.

Entrepreneurs too can glimpse new possibilities by ridding themselves of blocking assumptions. If we assume soap always comes in blocks, we will never be able to imagine it in liquid form. If we confine our thinking about crisps to potatoes, we will never imagine the possibility of parsnip and beetroot crisps. Likewise, when we think 'lock', we may automatically imagine 'key'. Locks may have keys but we have invented many different kinds of 'key', such as electronic cards. Many cities have broken the blocking assumption that big events such as football matches take place inside a stadium by opening up free space and exploiting the possibilities of wide-screen television.

TEN KEYS TO INNOVATION

The best way to coax ideas is to be systematic. Imagine that what follows is like a bunch of keys. Work through them one by one. Some may not be helpful but others may unlock entrepreneurial potential.

Imagine things that never were and ask, 'Why not?'

KEY 1: REINVENT THE FAMILIAR

One approach to inventing new ideas involves taking familiar products or services for which there is already a market and reinventing them. Take the aforementioned humble potato crisp. When I was a child, the only varieties on offer were 'plain' and 'cheese and onion'. There followed a flood of innovations. Likewise, the laptop computer introduced portability into a world dominated by desktop machines. Social entrepreneurs in the 19th and early 20th centuries who established the cooperative stores, and even pubs as cooperatives, were not anti-profit but challenged the idea of private appropriation. Boutique hotels offer guests services plus a personal touch that reduces the anonymity and loneliness of large hotels in large cities.

In order to see new possibilities, try questioning basic concepts and assumptions. What is a hotel? Is it a sleeping factory or a place where guests come to enjoy good food and relax in pleasant and secure surroundings?

av bab!

Ask silly questions.
The answers may be very rewarding.

Asking obvious (silly) questions can be extremely rewarding. For instance, why do guests need hotels? Wouldn't they rather be at home? These seemingly silly questions were the precursor to the development of timeshare apartments in cities such as London catering for the more affluent visitors where guests' personal effects are stored and laid in anticipation of visits to create a feeling of being 'at home'.

At the other end of the socio-economic scale, housing associations have made homes affordable by breaking the conventional assumption that ownership means that one must own a whole house. Instead, associations retain partial ownership and offer buyers the opportunity to acquire a percentage of the equity, thus enabling people who might otherwise be left behind to secure a toehold on the property ladder.

KEY 2: IMPROVE THE FAMILIAR

In the 19th century an entrepreneur named George Mortimer Pullman built opulent railway carriages and introduced innovations such as on-board catering and 'at seat' services in return for a supplement. Mortimer took ordinary train travel and made it better. The idea sold in developed countries all over the world and lives on in tours like the Orient Express.

Entrepreneurially minded farmers have also seen possibilities in organic meat and vegetables. They succeed by offering what supermarkets struggle to imitate, such as rare varieties, unusual recipes, exceptionally well-hung meats and so forth. Dyson vacuum cleaners are vacuum cleaners made better. Videoconferencing saves time, money and effort and helps to protect the environment. Yet it is not used as much as it could be because the equipment is cumbersome and temperamental. If it could be improved, videoconferencing might become the norm rather than the exception.

Tiptree would have been lost if they had challenged the big companies directly. Instead, they made jam and marmalade with a substantially greater proportion of fruit to sugar than the big manufacturers saw fit to offer and also offered a much wider range of flavours, such as ginger and pineapple in contrast to the more familiar strawberry and raspberry. Tiptree have since extended their approach to ketchups and chutneys.

KEY 3: REDUCE LOSS

One way of improving a product or a service is to reduce the loss that it imparts to a customer. The following are some examples of loss:

- queuing at a hotel checkout;
- waiting for a computer to 'boot up';
- the background 'hiss' the television makes;
- clothes that need washing;
- window frames that need painting;
- cars that need servicing;
- the weight of a lawnmower;
- waiting in a doctor's surgery;
- preparing a supermarket in readiness for customers;
- the time it takes to microwave a meal.

Loss refers to anything that imparts cost but no value. For instance, queuing at a hotel checkout means guests lose time. Some hotels employ extra staff at peak times to reduce the loss. (A surprising number don't.) Better still, some operate express checkouts where departing customers receive their bills under their doors during the night and report to checkout only if the bill is incorrect. All else being equal, where would you rather stay? And would you rather hump a heavy lawnmower over the grass or use one that floats over the surface? We can invent better soap powders and detergents but what customers really want is clean clothes. Tesco's decision to move to 24-hour opening was partly driven by the sheer cost of activities associated with opening up and shutting down stores in the morning and at night.

A famous example of reducing loss to the customer is the Dyson vacuum cleaner, which dispensed with the additional expense of buying dust bags. A more recent innovation that also reduces loss to the customer has been to abandon the traditional 'four-wheel' and mount the machine on a ball to improve efficiency and handling.

KEY 4: SOLVE PROBLEMS

Life is full of problems waiting to be discovered! I once stayed in a friend's house. I boiled an egg for breakfast and then realized that the house was devoid of eggcups. Only by trying to eat an egg off a plate did I realize how useful an eggcup is. Who invented it? Fountain pens that ran out of ink were a nuisance until someone invented cartridges. We never thought much about how messy and restricting wires are until Bluetooth technology arrived.

In order to solve problems you have to recognize their existence and then ask yourself what you can do about it. That means being willing to challenge the status quo and 'taken-for-granted' assumptions about what is acceptable and what can be changed. It means thinking about what 'could be' as distinct from what merely 'is'. It is the difference between asking 'why?' and 'why not?'.

Chad Varah, who founded the Samaritans in the early 1950s, noted that on average three people committed suicide every day in London. Was this an acceptable state of affairs? Was there nothing he could do? Chad Varah's starting point was to challenge the assumption that crisis counselling is necessarily a specialized task. His starting point was to assert that ordinary men and women with training in only a few basic principles could be effective and then to mobilize that potentially immensely powerful resource. More recently, some entrepreneurially minded companies thought seriously about the implications of diminishing reserves of oil and began to develop hybrid petrol/electric cars. The prototypes were frequently the butt of jokes, but people are no longer laughing.

KEY 5: TAKE WHAT NOBODY WANTS

'Where there's muck, there's brass.' As this homely Northern saying recognizes, fortunes have been built by entrepreneurs focusing upon what no one else wants – and not just hawking manure either!

The philosophical starting point rests in the notion of the empty. Try pouring coffee into a full cup. It will spill over and make a mess because the cup is already full. So, the cup is most useful when it is empty. Large, established businesses are likewise 'full'. They are full of products, full of commitments. Entrepreneurial potential resides not in competing head-on with giants but in exploring the empty space, the things that large organizations are not interested in.

A cup is most useful when it is empty.
(Lao Tzu)

The Post Office geared itself to receive pennies and ha'pennies saved by the thrifty poor – customers for whom the grand Victorian banks did not cater. More recently, the low-cost airline easyJet was launched from regional airports that the big airlines shunned, where landing fees were correspondingly cheap. The Naxos record company focused on older works that were out of copyright, and relatively unknown artists. (There is also a lesson for career building here as many of those artists are now well known.)

KEY 6: MAKE THE EXPENSIVE CHEAP

It is almost a cliché to cite Henry Ford's Model T car as an example of opening up an expensive entity to mass production. Happily, there are other examples in business history. The uniformly priced postage stamp facilitated mass communications. In the 1950s, Berni Inns made eating in restaurants possible for lower-income citizens. More recently, 'pay as you go' services have made mobile phones universally affordable.

Subtract, subtract and subtract again.

In school and higher education, the emphasis is upon adding to knowledge. In contrast, entrepreneurs subtract. Rowland Hill, who is credited with the invention of the postage stamp, got rid of a system of complicated tariffs based on weight and distance, and introduced a single uniform charge encapsulated in the stamp known as the 'Penny Black'. Berni Inns reduced the price of meals by removing tablecloths, thereby saving over £250,000 a year in laundry, and substituting table mats; by reducing the number of dishes on offer to cut the cost of inventory; and by keeping dishes simple so that they could be cooked and served by relatively inexpensive technicians rather than highly trained cooks. Although the Berni chain is long defunct, the underlying idea lives on in dining pubs. Indeed, dining pubs take the idea further as customers get their own drinks and order their own food, thereby cutting down on the need for waiting staff. Low-cost airlines have taken a similar approach by subtracting 'frills' such as meals. 'Pay as you go' mobile phone customers get a stripped-down version of the service afforded to contract customers.

KEY 7: GET THE PRICE RIGHT

Subtraction will make things cheaper but it will not help you decide how much to charge. It is not just a matter of making something affordable; it has to fit the customer's budget. This is where psychology can help.

Budgeting is a way of compartmentalizing resources either mentally in our heads or on paper. We use budgets to help control expenditure: 'so much for gas, so much for electricity' and so forth. Most of us carry around notional budgets in our heads. For example, we may decide that we will not pay more than, say, £20,000 for a car, or £9.99 for a paperback. Research by psychologists suggests that we are more likely to hesitate over buying something if it means breaking the budget.

Give people what they want at a price they will pay.

Note that I did not say 'if we cannot afford it'. The customer may be a millionaire but still resistant to paying more than £9.99 for a paperback book. In other words, if something is going to sell, the price must be within budget.

Economics also enters into the equation. Starbucks pay huge rents for their railway station kiosks, but that is not why their coffee is expensive. The coffee is expensive because the kiosks are strategically positioned where you and I, in a hurry and eager for a caffeine 'fix', will pay inflated prices. The rents are high because landlords know the value of the location. The same principle explains why food and drink in convenience stores adjacent to railway stations are more expensive than less conveniently located stores. Commuters value their time and will therefore pay a premium for convenience. Moral: charge what the customer will bear.

That means being careful not to overcharge. After eating an expensive and indifferent burger from a high street chain, Wayne and his brother decided to 'give it a go' by selling burgers, hot dogs and fried chicken from a mobile van on an outdoor market. They decided to undercut chains by selling at £3.69 instead of £4.60. It seemed foolproof, particularly as Wayne and his brother had gone to considerable trouble to create unique high-quality recipes, but no one bought. Wayne then reduced the price to match the typical market spend of £2.99. The result was astonishing, as Wayne recounts:

We gave two pieces of chicken, chips and a drink like you get at _____.
Where they were £4.60, we were on at £3.59 – but it just wasn't selling
even though the product's fantastic, absolutely fantastic. We couldn't
understand why it wouldn't go. So I says, 'It's the price.'

Me [sic] brother says, 'But we're a pound cheaper than _____.'

I said, 'I know, but... three pound fifty odd is nearly four quid.' So I said,
'Right! £2.99!'

Me [sic] brother said, 'it's too cheap', but we're still saleable – still
making decent money on it. So we put it on at £2.99 and within a week
trade went mad. '£2.99 for me dinner! We'll have that!'

The same recently happened in big business. When ASUS launched the
Eee with its 7-inch screen and internet capability for £199, trade went
mad. The product was originally designed for children but by happy
accident it gave adults what they wanted too at a price well within
budget.

KEY 8: ADD VALUE

Adding value is another possibility. The UK textile industry has largely
succumbed to foreign competition but there is still a market for speciality
cloth. In fact, there is actually a shortage of weaving capacity in the
United Kingdom. You can buy a box of Faber-Castell pencils in a nice
wooden box for around £70. A splendid way of adding value to a few
bits of wood! Luxury stationers Smythson have done a similar thing for
paper. Entrepreneurially minded scientists are working on inventions to
improve military combat dress. Existing suits of green and brown or
sand-coloured desert do a reasonably good job of providing camouflage.
They are detectable by the naked eye, however, particularly at close
quarters. Scientists are currently experimenting with scientific discover-
ies into how human vision works to add value by making suits that are
utterly invisible.

Another possibility is to repackage the mundane. There is nothing
special about a bag of Granny Smith apples. Imagine, however, receiving
rarer varieties packed in an attractive presentation box. You would probably be prepared to pay much more for the latter than the former, even
though they are all apples.

Adding value is the opposite side of the coin of reducing loss.
Customers will pay for mineral water in attractive bottles because it
means they can place the bottle directly on to the table and avoid having
to use a jug. This is why customers will pay more for two skinned
chicken breasts than for a whole chicken. The point is, cutting and

skinning adds value to the product out of all proportion to the cost of the labour involved.

KEY 9: INVENT A NAME

Branding & marketing

What would you like for lunch? How about a piece of cheese, a piece of celery, a bit of bread, and a dab of chutney?

You wouldn't like it all? In that case, how about a ploughman's lunch?

When I run this exercise with MBA students there are seldom any takers for the former, yet hands shoot up when I offer the latter! Which is odd, because they are the same thing...

We will probably never know the identity of the entrepreneurial genius who coined the term 'ploughman's lunch'. The lesson is that there is money to be made in giving things an attractive name.

In 1854, cholera erupted in the Soho area of London. A bright doctor named John Snow thought that the outbreak might be related to the water supply. He made a map of the area plotting the number of cases per household and marked the location of the wells. Dr Snow noticed that the highest density of cases centred upon a particular well, suggesting that this was the source of water contamination. Dr Snow tested his hypothesis by removing the pump handle. The number of cases then fell drastically, suggesting that his theory was correct.

Over a century later, in May 1981, Peter Sutcliffe (known as the Yorkshire Ripper) was convicted of murdering 13 women and seriously injuring 7 more between 1975 and 1980, though there may have been many other victims. Eventually, in late 1980, amid mounting concern over the police's continuing ineffectiveness, a special squad was formed to review the manhunt. A scientist attached to the team named Professor Stewart Kind was lying in his hotel bed unable to sleep for thinking about the case, when an idea suddenly struck him. Kind realized that the murderer would be under similar pressure to that faced by a wartime bomber; that is, to get home safely. Most of the attacks were committed in Leeds and Bradford with outliers in Huddersfield, Manchester, Halifax and Keighley. Professor Kind reasoned that the further away from the murderer's home an attack happened, the earlier in the evening it was likely to be because of the greater distance to home, in order to minimize the risk of detection. He used this information to plot the centre of gravity of the attacks – rather as the 19th-century physician identified the suspect well. The results pointed to halfway between the Shipley and Manningham areas – a very close approximation, as it turned out.

If Professor Kind had been involved in the investigation sooner, many lives might have been saved. In fact, Sutcliffe was arrested weeks later in Sheffield by two alert police officers making a routine enquiry. The technique pioneered by Professor Kind is now used by police forces all over the world, but it fell to an entrepreneurially minded American scientist to profit financially from the idea by developing dedicated software and, most importantly, giving the technique a name; 'geographical profiling'.

KEY 10: THE MASTER KEY

Ultimately, innovations stand or fall according to whether or not they gain (and retain) social acceptance. Some good ideas fail because people reject them. Screw caps on wine bottles are every bit as technically efficient as conventional corks and impart less loss to the customer, but only a few producers use them and then sometimes only on the slightly cheaper ranges. This is perhaps because consumers associate screw caps with poorer quality wines.

Sometimes there seems to be no logical reason for acceptance or rejection. Video-style telephone facilities are nothing new. They first appeared in the early 1970s but the idea was a commercial failure. Even with today's improved technology, mobile telephone companies struggle to sell the service. Conversely, text messaging facilities were added to mobile phones as an afterthought but they are actually more popular than voice calls. It seems bizarre when you consider the difficulties involved in 'typing' out a text message. Only a tiny minority of mobile phones embody QWERTY keyboards, yet customers do not seem to mind the tortuous process. And look around on a bus or a train and you will see that the market for iPods extends far beyond teenagers.

If the time is not right, an idea may stall. When venture capitalists were seduced by the so-called dotcom boom, they rejected many better propositions. Politics too can enter the equation. Entrepreneurs who have tried to sell ideas such as cooling caps that prevent hair loss in patients being treated for cancer found themselves up against the medical establishment. Although the caps added only £10 to the cost of treatment, doctors argued that they were too expensive. Conversely, there is little evidence that security cameras reduce crime, but now that we have them, there would probably be an outcry if they were removed.

Gaining acceptance may involve dilution. The Spanish tourist resort Benidorm was once a fishing village. Falling air travel costs prompted

patenting — locks up rival 'ideas'

the entrepreneurial mayor to develop (and ultimately overdevelop) the town as a holiday resort. The mayor succeeded, however, not by offering UK tourists authentic Spanish food and drink, but the familiar bacon and eggs plus the merest frisson of authenticity. Some Indian and Chinese restaurants (particularly in the early years) have also found dilution profitable.

It is possible to lose social acceptance as well as gain it, as evidenced, for example, by the downturn in the market for conventional light bulbs, battery-produced eggs and plastic carrier bags. Events of 11 September 2001 seriously undermined global chains like McDonald's and Burger King, particularly in Third World countries, as the terrorist attacks destroyed social belief in things American. On the other hand, it was good news for local street sellers.

As to what gains acceptance – that is anybody's guess! Gaining trust is important. Dell made home computers cheaper by selling through mail order, but it took years before customers learned to trust mail order. Indeed, Dell ended up paving the way for the rapid establishment of businesses such as Amazon and eBay.

Listening to customers can also help. This is where entrepreneurs have a head start over big business. Whereas executives sit in their offices all day studying statistics, entrepreneurs, particularly those at an early stage in their careers, are at the sharp end. They experience customer reactions first-hand. Ann, a young entrepreneur, planned to open a chain of shops. Lacking references and credentials, the only premises she could rent to open her first shop were in an economically deprived inner-city area. Ann invested a large portion of her precious capital in silver jewellery. Customer feedback soon told Ann she had made a fundamental mistake. Ann said:

> Lower working class want to buy gold. They believe that if they're wearing gold, they look worth more. Even if it's the cheapest, nastiest gold they can get, *they want gold*!

So she gave them gold – at £1.50 an item. It was indeed cheap and possibly nasty, but it sold.

Summary

1. Ideas for business are more likely to come via active search.

2. Start by questioning underlying concepts.

3. Look for hidden assumptions that may be restricting progress.

4. Ask yourself, 'Why?'

5. Then ask, 'Why not?'

6. Experiment with the 10 keys to innovation:
    - Reinvent the familiar.
    - Improve the familiar.
    - Reduce loss.
    - Solve problems.
    - Take what nobody wants.
    - Make the expensive cheap.
    - Get the price right.
    - Add value.
    - Invent a name.
    - Don't forget the master key.

2

Deciding to 'Give It a Go'

– how not to do it

I thought, 'What have I done? I've bought rubbish.'
(Jim, an experienced entrepreneur)

🔑 Key message: Why learn the hard way?

A good idea for business is important but it is not enough. Just as in academe there are interesting questions and there are researchable questions, in business there are good ideas and ideas that are good *and* commercially viable.

The statistics on new business start-ups are frightening. Fewer than 20 per cent survive beyond two years. Moreover, when new businesses collapse, the results are often financially and emotionally devastating. Nor are experienced entrepreneurs immune from failure. Almost all tell stories about deals that soured, about contracts that lost money and opportunities that became liabilities – sometimes with disastrous consequences.

business success rates

Yet many failures are avoidable.

Obviously, you will never know for certain whether an idea is viable until you try. It is axiomatic that all decisions involving uncertainty run the risk of failing. No matter how carefully you plan and research a prospective venture, there are no cast-iron guarantees of success. The trouble is, what defeats many fledgling – and experienced – entrepreneurs is not the hazards of 'war' so much as the certainties of common sense.

To be more precise, failure often reflects errors of judgement. Such errors are what psychologists call systematic. That is, we believe we know what causes them, how they are likely to bias decision making and how to correct them. Please read on; what follows could make all the difference.

THE ILLUSION OF CONTROL

Imagine choosing a lottery card. Which option would you prefer (assume the shopkeeper is honest): to accept a card from the shopkeeper or to choose the card yourself? Logically it makes no difference which option you choose. The statistical probabilities of winning are identical. Yet you may have elected to choose the card yourself because intuitively you feel you are more likely to win if you do.

Psychologists call it the illusion of control. The illusion of control refers to our innate tendency as human beings to overestimate our ability to influence outcomes – even those that are actually down to chance.

In 1982, distinguished psychologist Shelley Taylor published a fascinating book named *Positive Illusions*, which suggested, among other things, that depression might not actually be seeing things as worse than they are, but, rather, seeing them as they are. Taylor's thesis is that we are out of touch with reality to begin with! For example, according to Taylor, most people have an overly inflated idea of their own competence, as evidenced, for example, by our slavish adherence to the daily 'to do' list. Almost every time we compile such a list, says Taylor, we seriously overestimate what we can accomplish in a single day. Moreover, says Taylor, we never learn. Having accomplished only a fraction of the tasks that we set ourselves, undaunted we go and make another list!

Up to a point, illusions of control are a Good Thing. If you thought too deeply and seriously about all the risks involved in starting and running a business, you might never try. Indeed, it is often the realists who quit first when the going gets rough — precisely because they can see only too well that the odds are against them. Paradoxically, optimists may win through in the end because they have no idea of what they are up against!

But only up to a point! Ultimately there are concrete realities to be addressed. Hitler made this mistake when he invaded Russia. He insisted that the troops could fight effectively in sub-zero temperatures without proper winter clothing. No matter how much Hitler berated his generals, it made no difference. His tanks could not move without petrol. His soldiers could not march without sufficient food. Likewise, entrepreneurs need a cash flow: they need to sell enough to meet expenses, restock and perhaps repay loans. Where is the money going to come from?

THE OVERCONFIDENCE TRAP

These are vital questions. Yet overconfident entrepreneurs may not stop to ask them. Why else do people buy pubs that have already had a succession of owners who have gone bankrupt? They do it because they believe they can make a difference, though usually they just end up bankrupt too.

Overconfidence can manifest itself in other ways. Michael bought a business that he had worked in for five years. He knew (or should have known) that it was taking very little money; that was why the owner was selling it so cheaply. Instead of confronting the problem and thinking about whether and, if so, how he could achieve a turnaround, Michael simply put up a notice saying 'Under New Management', as if that alone would suffice. He lasted just 16 weeks.

DREAMING WITH DISCIPLINE

When I recount these stories to my MBA students, someone usually asks, 'Didn't they have a business plan?' In my experience, entrepreneurs who fail typically make one of three mistakes, namely:

1. They have no plan at all.
2. Their plan is not properly thought through.
3. They 'fiddle' the figures until the plan makes financial sense.

The mechanics of business plans are beyond the scope of this book. What I can say, however, is that, done properly, a plan is a good way of testing reality, thereby helping to avoid the overconfidence trap because the process of planning forces you to consider whether your ideas are practical. The trouble is that the most important element of the plan is ultimately guesswork. You can usually estimate costs with reasonable accuracy. More difficult is estimating how many customers there will be and how long it will take for the business to become established.

Starting a new venture, 'giving it a go', whether it is a completely new foray into business or branching out from an existing business, can be very exciting. When we feel strongly committed to something, we can develop blind spots, paying more attention to information that supports our preconceived notion while downplaying or even ignoring contradictory information. Some entrepreneurs go into business with no plan, no idea what to expect and therefore nothing to measure success or failure against. Others embark upon business with half a plan; as we shall see later in this chapter, with key elements such as cash flow projections missing. Another problem is what we call 'gaming'; increasing prices or bumping up the anticipated level of custom until it all makes sense – on paper, that is. It is only when the business starts to travel the rocky road of reality that those optimistic projects start to unravel.

Incidentally, once you become established in business, you may well receive requests from would-be and other established entrepreneurs for financial support. Some – a few – of these opportunities will be worth pursuing. The majority are likely to be 'no-brainers'. It was one of the Rothschilds, I think, who said that if he had pursued even a fraction of the opportunities that were offered to him, he would have been rapidly ruined. Treat such investment opportunities with healthy scepticism. Ask the same questions that a bank manager or venture capitalist would ask of you, such as:

- How much is the prospective owner proposing to invest in the idea?
- Who else is involved?
- At face value, does the idea seem credible?
- What market research has been conducted and with what results?
- How comprehensive and well thought out is the business plan?
- Does the prospective owner have the requisite skills and experience to run the business?

■ Does the prospective owner have the requisite energy and commitment to go the distance?

THE DANGERS OF MYOPIA

Fail to take account of the whole picture

Insufficient reality testing may result in myopia that prevents us from seeing a complete and accurate picture. For example, Sam explains the rationale for his first business − a franchised outlet selling trinkets costing £1:

Blind spots

> I think people will pay if cheap. There are other [similar] businesses [that] charge £5. £5 is too much for some people to pay − so I think that if I just charge £1 people will buy. First Saturday made £900.

At first blush, Sam's strategy appears sound: he is competing on price, with a clear rationale of appealing to the less affluent shoppers. Further probing reveals a fundamental flaw, however, as Sam has really only got half of a business plan. Sam again: 'Now is Tuesday and people only look, they no buy. Already they ask, "When is new stock coming in?"'

Given that the new stock only came in the previous day (Monday), the downturn seems ominous. The novelty value of the business has already passed and people are visiting not to buy but merely for entertainment. How will Sam fare the next Saturday, and the Saturday after that?

Myopia resides in failing to consider the other side of the equation. People may buy, but what about the rent of £500 a week plus business rates and all the other expenses? Sam needs to make £900 every Saturday just to cover expenses and replenish stock. Then he has an assistant to pay. Assuming he breaks even, he and his business partner receive nothing. Is that sustainable and, if so, for how long?

In business there are risks.
But there are also certainties.

The point is, none of this is hidden from Sam. No uncertainty surrounds the rent and other expenses. He has placed too much reliance upon his pricing strategy and not thought enough about the practicalities of implementing it.

Recall: a good idea for business is not enough. When Marcia was made redundant, she decided to turn a problem into an opportunity to exploit her specialist knowledge by opening a takeaway business selling exotic cuisine. In principle it was a promising scheme because it would be difficult for competitors to imitate. But Marcia too had only half a plan as she neglected cash flow and in particular the cost of supplies – until the business was under way. Marcia said:

> I was like, 'Oh my God! I didn't realize it would be so expensive.' Just the meat alone because we do special mutton: now mutton is not something that is easy to get hold of, and when you do get it, it's expensive. And we were buying that every single day – even though you're selling [sic]... it's every day you have to replace it, it's quite a lot of money.

Again there was no uncertainty about the price of mutton. Marcia ended up learning the hard way because she failed to think through in sufficient detail how the business would operate in practice. There is no substitute for mapping out an idea in detail. If you cannot afford to buy stock, the blunt reality is that you have no business.

It is also very important to research the local market. What is the going rate for goods and services? Another mistake made by Marcia was that in order for her to create a seemingly viable business plan, her prices were significantly above the average customer mental/financial budget. She then discovered that not enough people were buying her albeit delicious food, so she raised the price in order to meet her expenses but, in fact, only compounded her difficulties.

DENIAL

As human beings we are adept at hearing good news and equally adept at shutting out bad news. Since denial occurs unconsciously, we may believe that we have done our homework, asked all the right questions and weighed the answers. In fact, it may be that nothing is further from the truth.

Better to begin with doubts and end in certainties
than begin with certainties and end in doubts.

Carole ran a profitable business selling reconditioned televisions and videos. As new sets became cheaper, she realized that she needed to look elsewhere for the mainstay of her business. She decided to diversify into the 'one-hour' dry-cleaning business. It was an enormous investment but Carole was confident that it would succeed because there was a constant stream of passing trade and no competition nearby. Carole said:

> The people who sold it did not promise that it was going to make a fortune. They said that it was a good thing to augment a business that was already established. Everything that they said was true in actual fact. But I believed that being... where the footfall was so great, we couldn't fail. I felt that we were really on to a winner.

Notice what happens here. The company marketing the equipment behave ethically as they explain the limitations of the business. Carole, however, glossed over the point. The result is an enormous gap between expectations and reality concerning a critically important investment decision:

> I thought that [dry cleaning] would be a good money-spinner. In actual fact it wasn't – it was poor. It's very labour-intensive for little return... That was a huge gamble which did not pay off.

In fact, the business generated just enough money to cover the repayments on the loan. Carole said:

> We forgot the main thing about people. They'll see what they expect to see. And we were invisible... They didn't see because they didn't expect to see... You will get people coming to you, after four years – people that you see day in, day out would bring me a suit to clean and they would say, 'Never noticed you here – didn't realize that you did dry cleaning.' I paid £100,000 for the equipment and I got £1,500 for it when I sold it. So that was a major blow to my finances.

It is a speculative point but we may be most susceptible to making erroneous decisions like Carole's when things are not going well and an apparent solution to our problems suddenly appears. Again, speculatively, we may also be propelled into bad decisions when we have been searching unsuccessfully for a solution for a long time and end up pouncing upon something (anything) just to end the pain of indecision.

TOO GOOD TO LOSE?

Some successful entrepreneurs claim to rely solely upon intuition when making important decisions. In other words, they dispense with analysis and certainly never bother with writing business plans. We will see in the next chapter that intuition does have an important role to play in decision making. The danger I wish to highlight here, however, is that what we call intuition may be merely wishful thinking. If, like Carole, you believe that an idea can hardly fail, treat that belief as a danger signal. Luck does play a part in business but be aware that susceptibility to myopia is also heightened when an opportunity seems to be too good to miss. This is because we are liable to be dazzled by all the advantages of the idea and therefore neglect to probe the potential hazards. Sue was offered a large consignment of cheap T-shirts. On paper it looked an admirable proposition. Buy for 25p and sell for £2.99. Before reading on, pause awhile and evaluate this proposition. Is it a good idea? What snags can you think of?

'I won't ever go down that road again,' said Sue.

'Why?' I asked. 'Didn't they sell?'

Sue replied:

Oh yeah, we sold 'em. We sold 'em all day long. I had this stack on t'floor. You think how much you've got to sell at £2.99 to make £400 and how much work there is. A major mistake; we did sell 'em, yeah, but with the effort that went into selling at £2.99 I could have gone out and sold a bloody Ferrari quicker... Then everybody wanted everything... for £2.99. So, it killed everything else. [People] came up, 'Is that £2.99, is that £2.99?' DOH! And we're still getting it now. I won't ever go down that road again. Never!

Stop!
Think!
How might this decision play out in practice?

Faced with a seemingly windfall opportunity, Sue seized it without thinking about how the decision might play out in practice. She probably could not have foreseen that this 'Del Boy' opportunity would 'kill everything else', but a grain of imagination would have shown the floor piled up with crates of T-shirts, and a calculation on the back of an envelope would have revealed how much work would be involved in making £400 and given Sue pause to question whether this was such a good idea after all.

OVERREACH

An opportunity is an opportunity if you can deliver on it.
Otherwise it is a liability.

Culturally we are conditioned to make the most of our opportunities. The proverb warns, 'he who hesitates is lost' – as we may never have the chance again. While this is good advice, entrepreneurs should be careful not to overreach themselves. Success is built not only on the opportunities we take but also on those that we have the courage to turn away.

Richard worked in local government as a solicitor. The opportunity arose for him to buy a high street practice cheaply from a retiring solicitor. The offer was genuine but again, can you see the risk?

Richard seized the chance and bought the business. The decision was a disaster because he had no experience of running a practice. He knew nothing about staff management, maintaining accounts, sending out bills and so forth. Moreover, having worked mainly in planning and social services law, Richard had no experience of crime and matrimonial work – the core business of high street practices. Becoming more and more stressed, Richard began putting more complex cases aside. He was eventually reported to the Law Society by another firm, was censured and gave up being a solicitor altogether.

Notice what happens here. The opportunity is so dazzlingly good that Richard never stops to think about what is involved until he is well and truly submerged in the practice. By then it is too late as the business is already out of control.

Don't try to run before you can walk.

Expansion is almost every entrepreneur's goal but it brings new challenges. It is very important to ensure that you are competent to meet those challenges before embarking upon a new phase of development. By competent I mean do you possess the deep foundational technical and financial security that will enable you to sustain what is basically a period of turbulence and moving out into uncharted waters? In politics, being clever is not enough to guarantee success; politicians also require weight and gravitas. The same is true for business development. Continuous expansion is rarely sustainable. Expansion should be punctuated by phases of consolidation.

Overly rapid and overly ambitious expansion can result in firms overreaching themselves. The managers of a small brewery employed just 35 people and brewed only a few barrels every week. Demand for good-quality beer was growing and they began to think about expanding production on-site when the chance arose to buy a redundant brewery – cheap. It seemed like a tremendous opportunity because it offered an eightfold increase in capacity for much less money than the other option of doubling on-site capacity. The management team decided to buy even though a non-executive director resigned over the decision.

Again the decision was a disaster. The elderly boiler and lifting gear kept breaking down. The waste treatment plant had to be replaced at considerable expense when the government introduced new laws. Most seriously, money started flowing out much faster than it flowed in, as the decision makers had not realized that the profit margins on large-scale production were much thinner than those on more tightly controlled small-scale production. A cash flow crisis resulted in a forced merger and the end of the management team's cherished independence.

If the brewery managers had only paused for long enough to rehearse how the new business model might operate in practice, the danger might have been more apparent. Instead, they were seduced by the seemingly fantastic opportunity, so they never considered the possible snags. A member of the management team said afterwards:

> Really, we seized an opportunity rather than made a planned decision... we felt we could hardly turn it [the purchase of the brewery] down. We were planning to spend £150,000 expanding our own brewery and the acquisition only cost £115,000.[1]

The brewery managers thought they were making a good decision based on their knowledge of the industry. The mistake was that they saw the similarities between the two operations (both brewed beer) but not the critical differences. Richard too saw the similarities between working in local government and entering private practice (he would still work as a solicitor) but not the vitally important differences. Psychologists call it the representativeness heuristic. The weighty terminology need not detain us. It simply means that the way in which the human brain processes information can be systematically biased. That is, we may notice the similarities between one case and another but not potentially important, if sometimes subtle, differences between cases. Consequently, we may believe that we know what we are doing when our knowledge is an illusion. The way to counter this form of bias is to conduct a rigorous analysis. If A and B seem similar, search for the differences. Then, having identified the differences, think hard about the implications.

What exactly are you buying?

In Richard's case, at least the opportunity was genuine. By contrast, David won the lottery and decided to fulfil his ambition to become a business owner. He paid £150,000 to buy a company that installed security cameras. When he examined his purchase in more detail, however, he discovered that it consisted merely of a name and an advertisement in a newspaper. The late media tycoon Robert Maxwell accomplished a similar feat of ingenuity when he sold Pergamon, the publishers. When the purchasers unwrapped their multi-million-pound acquisition, they too discovered that it was almost as hollow as David's security firm.

Caveat emptor! Let the buyer beware! There may be many advantages in buying an established business including an existing product line, embedded technology, a full order book, a good reputation and so forth. Yet be careful about paying out large sums of money for goodwill. In particular, be sure about what you are actually paying for and whether it is worth the asking price or anywhere near it.

THE EXPERIENCE TRAP

Richard and David were new to business. The brewery managers and those buying Pergamon were all experienced – yet they too made mistakes. Psychologists call it the experience trap. Firefighters are most likely to be killed not when they are new to the job but when they have been in it for about 10 years. This is because experienced firefighters develop a false confidence in themselves based on the belief that they have seen it all before.

---

*Never forget what made you successful to
begin with.*

Experience can likewise work against entrepreneurs. Jim discovered this
to his cost. Over the years he built a small but thriving chain of butcher's
shops. He noticed that the shop next door to his main outlet was always
busy with customers queuing out on to the pavement. When the owner
decided to retire, Jim outbid all competitors to acquire this apparent
'goldmine'. After the sale was agreed, Jim took a closer look at his new
acquisition. The result was a severe shock. The fixtures and fittings –
even the knives – were worn out and virtually useless. Jim said, 'I
thought, "There's nothing here; we'll have to pull the lot down – just
throw everything away and... completely rebuild it."'

Worse was to follow. Jim then asked the seller about the takings:

I had said to him [the seller], 'What sort of money should I expect to be
looking at for takings?'

He said, 'On a good week, £350 to £400 pounds. On a poor week say
£300 pounds.'... [Then] he said, 'Good luck with it in the future', and off he
walked.

I remember standing there, I were looking at this feller walking into the
distance – and I thought, 'What have I done here? I've bought rubbish...
I've got a shop in there that's doing like 15, 16 hundred a week and on a
good week this one does 4 hundred if I'm lucky!'

It was what Jim had *not* done that brought him to grief. When he was
younger and less certain, he would first have inspected the accounts of
his putative acquisition. He would have had a good look round the shop.
Instead, Jim took a short cut. He saw the long queues and concluded that
the shop must be profitable. He never stopped to think whether there
might be another explanation for the queues, for example that not
enough staff were employed, and/or ruined knives meant that it took
shop assistants longer to serve customers.

The danger with sustained success is that we interpret it as confirma-
tion of our competence. More specifically, research by psychologists has
shown that we tend to attribute our successes to our innate abilities and
our failures to bad luck. Such self-serving attributions can lead to blind
spots as we may not learn from our failures, and we may come to believe
we are invulnerable, not seeing that some of our success reflects luck
rather than good judgement.

ATTRIBUTION BIASES.

Moreover, success need not be accompanied by fireworks and symphony orchestras to delude us. Running a reasonably profitable business day in, day out counts as sustained success and is enough to inculcate complacency. Complacency is dangerous because research into gambling behaviour has shown that players who experience early wins in games of chance tend to bet more subsequently; success makes them feel more confident and therefore more inclined to take risks. By the same token, successful and complacent entrepreneurs may start taking short cuts. Like Jim, they may decide there is no longer any need to bother with writing out business plans, or asking questions, analysing their options and all the other decision tools. In other words, they dispense with all the things that made them successful in the first place.

Summary

1. All decisions involving uncertainty entail risk.

2. Many failures could be avoided, however, if entrepreneurs conducted sufficient reality testing beforehand.

3. Failure usually results from overconfidence and/or biased information processing.

4. The risks of misjudgement are heightened when an opportunity seems too good to lose.

5. Experience offers no immunity from error. In fact, it can make things worse.

NOTES

1. Cited in Wilson, D C, Hickson, D J and Miller, S (1996) How organizations can overbalance: decision overreach as a reason for failure, *American Behavioral Scientist*, **39** (8), 995–1010 at p 1003

3

Optimal Solutions

– how to choose between alternatives

The essence of the ultimate decision remains impenetrable to the observer – often, indeed, to the decider himself... There will always be the dark and tangled stretches in the decison-making process – mysterious to even those who may be intimately involved.
(John F Kennedy, former US president)

Key message: Good decisions combine head and heart

In theory, decision making proceeds as follows. Having identified a problem, the decision makers first remind themselves of their goals. Next they generate all possible alternatives and then compare the likely results of those alternatives with their goals. Finally, they choose the option that promises to be the best match to the goal.

The joke in academe is that this prescriptive model of optimal decision making actually describes what does *not* happen. Indeed, if choosing between alternatives were so simple, this book and many others would be redundant. The point is, even if we had the time to generate a near-exhaustive list of alternatives, our problems are only just beginning because what makes decision making hard (and interesting) is that because the future is unknown, we cannot be certain what to do for the best.

Yet we are not completely helpless – by any means. Some entrepreneurs claim to make decisions purely on emotional reaction or 'gut feel'. Indeed, contrary to what analytical models of decision making might suggest, emotion is an important factor in choosing between alternatives. Yet as we saw in Chapter 2, emotional influences can produce disastrous decisions.

That is not the same as saying that decisions based mainly upon reason and analysis are inherently superior. In fact, they can turn out to be just as bad as decisions driven purely by emotion! My task in writing this chapter is to persuade you that the trick of effective decision making is to listen to what *both* intellect *and* emotion are telling you.

SIX THINKING HATS

A powerful but simple tool for analysing alternatives is Edward de Bono's so-called thinking hats.[1] De Bono devised the technique for management teams whereby each member of the team would don a different-coloured hat according to their role in the evaluation process. It works just as well for individuals. You can conduct the exercises that follow in your head but you may find it useful to think with a pen in your hand and to keep a record of your thinking so that you can study and reflect upon the finer points of your analysis at leisure.

1. Blue hat: 'thinking about thinking' – what are you trying to achieve from the process?
2. Red hat: emotion – how do you feel about the idea? No justification is required here, just raw emotion and intuition.
3. White hat: what information do you need to make a decision?
4. Black hat: what are the risks and what is likely to happen in the future?
5. Yellow hat: taking a positive view, what is the best possible scenario? Give reasons for your answer.
6. Green hat: looking for new ideas and new ways of doing things – where could I go from here?

It is usually best to start with the blue hat. Donning the blue hat means being clear about what you hope to achieve by thinking about alternatives. For example:

- 'I need to decide which, if any, of the six premises I have inspected I am going to rent.
- 'I need to decide whether to continue paying for warehouse space to hold paper records or whether to scan the whole lot into a computer and move to electronic holdings.'
- 'I need to decide whether to take the offer of voluntary redundancy.'
- 'I need to decide whether to take up the offer of going into partnership.'
- 'I need to think about what opportunities there are for expansion.'

Jean was happy in her job as a classroom teacher. A friend asked her to go into business with her, running an agency for supply teachers. Beginning with the blue hat, Jean decided she would use the technique to help her decide whether to take the opportunity. She then used the red hat to express her feelings about the idea, which were a mixture of excitement and fear. Next she tried the yellow hat to map out the advantages. Not least of these were the possibilities it would open up. It could be a route out of the classroom and the daily grind of teaching. Jean then applied the black hat to examine the risks and the possible downside. These were uncertainty, loss of pension rights, and possible barriers to re-entering teaching if the venture failed. She also wondered whether she might miss teaching and school life. Jean then applied the green hat to expand the possibilities. 'I am happy as a teacher now,' said Jean to herself, 'but how will I feel in 5 or 10 years' time – ground down, stressed out?' Jean then considered another possibility: should she stay in her present job and think about applying for a headship or moving into administration? Jean then applied the white hat and realized that she needed to know more about the idea. For instance, could her friend guarantee a salary and pension?

SHORT CUTS

It is not always necessary to use all of the hats. Particular problems require different types of thinking.

What is impossible in your own life?
What would make a big difference to you if it were possible?

The 'six thinking hats' tool is not just about avoiding bad decisions. It is about uncovering possibilities in propositions that we might otherwise reject out of hand as negative or too risky. Stephen was a partner in a large firm of surveyors. He was offered early retirement. His initial reaction was negative ('why me?'). Stephen wondered if he were the victim of a sinister conspiracy. After the initial reaction subsided, Stephen realized that he might have been asking the wrong question. That is, instead of saying, 'why me?' he might have done some white hat thinking and asked, 'How much is it worth?' He might then have donned the yellow hat and tried to compile a list of advantages of being retired. If the list were a short one, then retirement might not be a good idea after all. Alternatively, Stephen might don the green hat and turn a problem into an opportunity. What could he do in retirement if he had enough money? Stephen eventually decided to retire if, and only if, the financial package offer was adequate for him to do those things he had never before thought about.

Yellow hat thinking is also about finding the proverbial silver lining. Even in the most miserable unlooked-for situations, there are possibilities waiting to be uncovered if only we stop to think about them. Indeed, the impetus to becoming an entrepreneur is often forced redundancy.

Green hat thinking is expansive. It involves thinking about what could be. Mont Blanc may be best known for their pens, which also double up as status symbols. The company has done some successful green hat thinking, however, in thinking about how to exploit the brand without overexploiting it, and has made successful incursions into selling watches, luxury leather goods and fragrances. By contrast, some Swiss watchmakers seem to have been slow to don the green hat. It is only recently, for example, that the exclusive brand Patek Philippe has turned its attention seriously to selling watches to women. It has so far not offered the market pens, luxury leather goods and fragrances, or attempted to exploit the brand in other ways, for example by linking the name with luxury makes of cars such as Bentley and Ferrari, as other watchmakers have seen fit to essay.

'Greens' and 'yellows' are also useful in thinking about what an idea might evolve into. In the early 1960s, Bruce was asked whether he would like to invest in a new type of business, namely one where instead of being served from behind a counter, shoppers pushed trolleys around and chose items for themselves and then paid at something called a 'checkout'. Bruce shook his head. 'It'll never catch on,' he said. Thus did he turn down the opportunity to become a director of Asda. The moral of the story: not enough yellow and green hat thinking.

Not enough white hat thinking, either. If Bruce had thought about the financial logic underpinning the idea behind this newfangled idea (white hat thinking), he would have realized that this new business model offered potentially powerful economies of scale – savings that could be passed back to shoppers. Green hat thinking might have revealed the generative possibilities of the idea, such as the attraction of having many products under one roof. Yellow hat thinking might have helped him to foresee the possibilities of 'cloning' and all that that implied.

Take your time.

Bruce decided in haste and repented at leisure. Some decisions have to be made quickly, but whenever possible, take your time. Time is particularly important in facilitating green hat thinking because it can suggest possibilities that might not be immediately apparent.

Sally inherited a clothes shop that made very little money. Her first instinct was to sell it. Then she began to consider the possibilities. Donning the green hat, Sally realized that there was a gap in the market between what licensed sex shops provide and the softer approach offering a frisson of sexual suggestion (with no licence required) and providing a personal service. Sally decided to experiment with mingling shirts, blouses and underwear with some more imaginative lines and by offering a sympathetic service. The experiment succeeded. Soon Sally was soon receiving recommendations from far and wide. She says:

> Put it this way, if somebody's got a wallet and they've got some money in it, I will take it. You know, bottom line: I am in business and I will take it. But I will give them the best service that I can give them. And we get... transvestites. Well, guys, obviously – what sort of a bra can I put this in? I don't laugh at them. I'm fascinated actually. But I think they come because I say, 'Well, if yer putting them thongs on, where do you tuck your bits?'
>
> And they say, 'What?!'

But how do you learn if you don't ask?

And they don't get embarrassed because I'm not laughing. I'm genuinely interested in what they do. And then somebody'll say to somebody, 'Go up there. They won't laugh at you, they'll actually help you.'

EXPLORING THE SNAGS

According to Edward de Bono, most decisions fail because of insufficient black hat thinking. No matter how tantalizing the opportunity, you should always explore the risks and possible downside. In the previous chapter, this is what the brewery managers and Richard the solicitor failed to do.

That said, begin by considering certainties before worrying about risks. For instance, if you buy a north-facing house, no amount of wishful thinking will make the property suddenly jump round and face south. If a business is located 200 kilometres away, that journey is not suddenly going to shrink to 20 kilometres. Immediately you open a business, money will start to flow out. American Express made this mistake when they diversified from issuing charge cards to issuing credit cards. The former were payable at the end of every month and in any case only available to persons meeting rigorous income requirements, whereas the latter involved longer-term loans and were available to lower-income groups. The increased risk was obvious enough, but the company failed to take due account of it and lost money on customer defaults accordingly.

If I do this, what will definitely happen?

Now that we uncovered potential problems, the next question is, can you cope? Be specific: if you are opening a business, where is the money for rent, rates and so forth to come from? How long can you afford to make those payments? Can you arrange credit facilities for essential supplies? If so, will they be adequate to tide you over until the business becomes established? If some of the rooms in the premises face south, would they suffice for your main needs?

Emphatically, the existence of risks and problems need not be a reason to reject an opportunity. The question is whether you can de-risk the venture or take counter-measures. Richard might have prospered if he had taken an experienced solicitor into partnership with him or entered into a consultancy arrangement. The brewery might have survived as an independent entity if the management team had opted for a modest increase of production instead of reaching out for a huge upsurge. The brewery's managers neglected to ask important questions such as how they were going to sell all the beer they produced and how they would finance upfront payments due to Customs & Excise.

REFRAME

Is the bottle half full or half empty? The answer depends on how you frame it! Framing refers to mathematically equivalent expressions. What is interesting, however, is that although half-full and half-empty bottles are mathematically equivalent, psychologically they are not. The former expression evokes positive reactions, the latter negative. For instance, if we say that an expensive drug for treating cancer has a 2 per cent success rate, the prospects sound much more optimistic than if we say the failure rate is 98 per cent. We are therefore more likely to question an idea that has a 98 per cent chance of failure than one that has a 2 per cent chance of success. We might well invest in the latter before we invest in the former! To counter this form of bias, reverse the framing. If a proposition is presented positively, see how it appears when framed negatively and vice versa.

Reframing can be applied in different ways to put ideas into perspective. Peter had founded a successful business selling camping gear. He was keen to expand. A friend owned a shop in another town. The shop sold second-hand office equipment and was not doing very well. The friend offered to sell some of Peter's camping gear in his shop. The friend suggested splitting the rent 50/50. Peter was excited by the possibility because he saw it as a low-risk opportunity to achieve an important goal. Once he thought about it, however, and reframed the problem, he realized it was also an invitation to pay half of his friend's rent. Peter did reject the idea and instead negotiated a lower rent. In fact, after six months Peter ended up moving his gear out of the shop as the experiment was clearly not working.

SHOWSTOPPERS

You can seek for perfection but you will rarely find it. A form of pragmatic thinking is to consider fitness for purpose. In other words, will it do?

Be careful about making compromises. According to the proverb, half a loaf is better than none. If you are hungry, yes. Otherwise, compromise may be dangerous. It is the difference between an opportunity and a liability.

Imagine opening a sandwich bar. Passing trade is imperative. The only premises available to rent are just round the corner from the high street. You may be tempted to 'give it a go'. After all, it is very close to your ideal of the high street. This is not a sensible compromise but a recipe for disaster. You may say, 'it will do to get started', or 'I have to start somewhere', or 'I will never get started'. I understand your anguish, but would you take your life savings and burn them? That is precisely what you are being invited to do here because the odds are so heavily against you. By definition, passing trade rarely turns corners; you might as well be trying to sell sandwiches on Mars for all the good it will do. The offer is unfit for purpose, so reject it.

Incidentally, I think this is why many successful entrepreneurs seem arrogant. Show them something or try to sell them an idea and they may respond brashly, 'That's no good to me.' Successful entrepreneurs know what they need to be successful and they have the patience and resilience to search for it.

FACT, NOT ASSUMPTION

It is vital to distinguish between fact and assumption. This may seem obvious, but we make assumptions all the time, and frequently without recognizing the fact. Every time we switch on the kettle we expect the water to boil, but it is an assumption nevertheless. Every time we board a train we assume it will take us to the place marked on the destination board, but it is an assumption. As the brewery managers discovered to their cost, an eightfold expansion in beer production did not, as they seem to have tacitly assumed, mean an eightfold expansion in profits. The law of diminishing marginal returns applies.

Crystal and her partner decided to open a Chinese takeaway business. The plan was to convert premises in a row of terraced houses. The premises had previously been a newsagent's. There was a gas tap in the kitchen. This was important, because running a successful takeaway means being able to produce food quickly. Electricity is almost useless for this purpose. It was only when Crystal applied to have the gas reconnected that she discovered the tap was defunct. The gas supply had been permanently disconnected long ago. By then, the pair had invested heavily in converting the premises. Given the presence of the gas tap, it was reasonable to assume a supply of gas to the premises but it was an assumption nonetheless, and wrong.

One way of differentiating between different types of information is to distinguish between:

- know for certain;
- unsure;
- assumed.

Interestingly, it is the 'known' facts that are often the most dangerous category of information because, like the gas tap, when tested they turn out to be mere assumptions.

Search for the hidden, rather more subtle assumptions. 'Keen to Sell' moved their estate agency from a fairly large town to a smaller one just 8 kilometres away. The partners thought it was a low-risk move because they had already built up a substantial business. As they saw it, they were merely swapping offices. Yet the decision almost bankrupted them. Far from merely relocating, they ended up starting from scratch, and their resources were barely adequate to see them through the initial financially lean phase of re-establishing themselves.

No matter how sure you are of something – check to make assurance doubly sure.

If Barings had done that, they might still be in existence. Generally speaking, higher profits in investment banking mean higher risks. Yet the managers of Barings Bank were not in the least bit worried when Nick Leeson's alleged profits began to outstrip those of the entire organization because they knew that Leeson's contracts were matched. Matched contracts mean that a contract with one party to buy was matched with an equal and opposite contract with another party to sell and vice versa. Peter Norris, Barings' chief executive, who chaired the committee that supposedly monitored Leeson's trading, said, 'Discussion... started with a reconfirmation that all our positions were fully matched. That premise was never doubted.'

The media subsequently speculated that Barings must have known about Leeson's entrepreneurial trading strategy and maybe even conspired with him. In fact, recorded transcripts of conversations between various members of the bank's management point to the complete opposite; that is, Barings felt secure in the knowledge that Leeson's trades were matched. That premise was never doubted even though the bank's future rested upon it, and even though, latterly, markets in the Far East were ablaze with rumours suggesting that Barings was incurring massive exposure to a mystery customer. It was only when Leeson mysteriously disappeared that Barings examined his accounts and discovered that Leeson's trades were not matched at all. In fact, they were completely open, exposing Barings to catastrophic risk, and Leeson's mystery customer was none other than Barings itself.[2]

ASKING THE RIGHT QUESTIONS

Part of the art of white hat thinking is asking the right questions. But how do you know the right questions to ask? Self-help starts with identifying what you don't know. The trouble is, you don't always know what you *don't* know. Experience teaches, but for the inexperienced this is where a mentor can be enormously helpful. Failing that, try thinking about what you are likely to meet, and consider the sort of questions that might arise.

For example, imagine that you have opened a successful restaurant or hotel. You then decide you would like to develop a franchised business. Try to think through what steps you would need to take in pursuit of your ambition.

Key steps to building a franchise

■ Protect trade name as a registered trade mark in Europe.
■ Define features that have made your enterprise successful.
■ Consider what methods and standards on design, quality, operations management and brand you need to teach franchisees.
■ Determine what systems you will need to have in place to attract franchisees. For example, if your franchise is a hotel, will you offer a computer-based reservations system to support the entire chain?

■ Develop a market concept that offers something new and interesting.

■ Determine what fees you will charge and other contractual requirements.

How many issues did you pick up on?

Asking the right questions becomes a habit of mind. Start by searching for the keystone question; that is, the central issue from which other questions flow. Study this list and it will become obvious that there is more to developing a franchise than merely replicating an existing business in another location. Notice, however, that they all flow from one central question, namely: what is it *precisely* that you intend to franchise? That is the keystone question.

WEIGHING UP ALTERNATIVES

A complementary technique for weighing up alternatives is the even swap method. The technique works, as Benjamin Franklin observed, by finding where the balance lies by examining 'pros' and 'cons' simultaneously. For example, if you are looking at two sets of premises and both face south (an important objective), then on that parameter there is nothing to choose between them. One has a big garden that could be turned into a car park. The other has outbuildings that could be converted as the business expands. Since both facilities are equally important to you, they cancel each other out, so you eliminate them. Keep repeating the process of elimination on all the important parameters until you are left with residual advantages. In other words, what, on balance, remains points to the optimal choice.

KILLER APPLICATION

You can short-circuit this process by concentrating upon the 'killer application'. The phrase refers to the pivotal goal, the one thing that really matters. It is an intelligent short cut to optimal decision making — provided it is used carefully. The BlackBerry is sparse on features

compared with other personal digital assistants (PDAs). I chose it in pref-
erence to numerous other possibilities for one reason and one reason
only, namely the tried and tested 'push' e-mail service – a decision I
have never regretted.

THE ENIGMA OF EMOTION

Supposing you have donned all the hats, weighed up 'pros' and 'cons',
and yet you are still undecided? Supposing the 'killer application' makes
the decision obvious and yet you are unsure? Or supposing analysis
reveals that there is little to choose between the alternatives? Or supposing that you have made a decision that is logical and rationally defensible but does not feel right?

This is the time to listen to what your emotions are telling you. Revisit
your red hat thinking. Emotions are crucial to good judgement because
we have to live with the consequences of our decisions.

Let emotion have the casting vote.

Elaine runs a consultancy specializing in helping small businesses to
market their products and services. She had always wanted to be a
magistrate. The selection process was long and searching. Elaine had
hardly opened the envelope containing the certificate of appointment
from the Lord Chancellor when she began to have doubts. It was partly
the time commitment: could she really juggle so many days? Then there
was the mandatory training requirement and performance appraisal.
That felt like a heavy price to pay for the privilege of being able to use
the designatory letters JP (Justice of the Peace).

Elaine felt torn. Then she looked at her red hat scribble, which
included words like 'anger', and she realized that being a magistrate
would impose restrictions upon her freedom. No more riding her bicycle
for a few metres on the pavement, and she would forever be required to
drive within the speed limit. 'If you feel like that now,' said her friend Pat,
who had been a magistrate for many years, 'you probably won't feel any
better once you start sitting.' Elaine decided it was not for her after all.

Do what you never expected to do.

Andrew owns a software company. He specializes in designing programs to help public service organizations detect fraud and corruption. He was offered the opportunity to tender for a contract in Afghanistan – a project connected with suppressing the illegal narcotics trade. Andrew was confronted with a dilemma. Apart from the physical danger, his black hat thinking raised questions about breaking out of his comfort zone. Yet his yellow and green hat thinking were both positive. It would be new experience and could open up new possibilities. White hat thinking was also positive. Andrew carefully and systematically compared the contractual requirements with his own skills and experiences and discovered a near-perfect correlation, so he was confident that he was capable of delivering – confidence born of fact, not dreams. He decided to let the red hat have the casting vote. It said, 'warm', 'sunny', 'exciting', 'FREEDOM! Free at last!!' Revisiting his red hat thinking, Andrew realized that although in practice he would actually have less freedom because he would be working behind a gated compound, his emotions were really telling him that his present business represented something of a rut that he needed to escape from. So, despite his reservations, he took a chance and eventually became an adviser to governments – something that would never have happened if he had remained within his comfort zone.

The point is, when you are making decisions, your 'head' will take you only so far. To make a good decision, you also have to analyse and weigh the possibilities, but you also have to listen to what raw emotion is telling you. So if, once you have donned the hats and analysed your spreadsheets, two options emerge as more or less equal, but one attracts you emotionally more than the other (even if the pull is only very slight), then that is the option to choose, because your emotions are telling you something very important.

Summary

1. Good decisions combine emotion and rigorous analysis.

2. Try Edward de Bono's six thinking hats:
   - blue: purpose of thinking;
   - red: raw emotion;
   - yellow: advantages;
   - green: possibilities;
   - black: risks and difficulties;
   - white: information needed to make a decision.

3. Most decisions fail through insufficient black or white hat thinking.

4. Insufficient yellow and/or green hat thinking can mean lost opportunity.

5. Distinguish between 'known', 'unclear' and 'assumed'.

6. Beware the known facts as they may turn out to be assumption.

7. All else equal, give raw emotion thinking the casting vote.

NOTES

1. See de Bono, E (2000) *Six Thinking Hats*, Penguin, London
2. Further discussed in Drummond, H (2008) *The Dynamics of Organizational Collapse*, Routledge, London

4

Decisions about Future Investments

– the sunk costs trap

Don't hold on to...

(The Buddha)

 Key message: Base decisions on future pay-offs, not past costs

- Your broadband connection has failed and you desperately need to restore it. You have been 'on hold' on the telephone helpline for five minutes, costing 60p a minute. How long do you continue waiting?
- Your investments have halved in value. Should you keep them or sell?
- You are converting an old mill into a block of flats. The once buoyant property market has collapsed. Should you finish the project?

Being on hold on the telephone, faltering share prices and a changing market − all of these problems share three features, namely that:

- you have made an investment in anticipation of results;
- results have yet to materialize;
- you must decide whether to quit or continue.

The dilemma is that if you quit all the time, money and effort invested in your venture will count for nothing. As with drilling for oil and finding a dry well, your investment has become merely an expense.

Yet if you persist, you may simply end up making things worse. Supposing the call centre does not operate a queuing system; you could be kept waiting indefinitely while costs mount. If shares are in free fall, should you cut your losses immediately?

SUNK COSTS

One factor that should *not* influence such decisions except in special circumstances is the amount already invested in the venture − known as past or, as I shall call them, sunk costs. Sunk costs should be ignored because they cannot influence future outcomes.

If this suggestion sounds absurdly wasteful, the following simple scenario will illustrate the point. Say you decide to turn your living room into a corner shop. The conversion costs are £30,000. The business generates an income of about £200 for a 70-hour week. After two or three years you begin to tire of the long hours and meagre returns. If you closed the shop and took a job stocking supermarket shelves, you could earn £350 for a 40-hour week.

Assuming your goal is to maximize your income and quality of life, you would be £150 a week better off working in the supermarket, and have a lot more free time. Moreover, it becomes obvious that the £30,000 invested in the shop is irrelevant when you reframe the problem as a choice between earning £2.86 per hour in the shop or earning £8.75 per hour in the supermarket.

THE SUNK COSTS TRAP

Intellectually, that decision makes itself. However, research by psychologists suggests that, emotionally, sunk costs can exert a powerful hold.

Part of the problem of letting go of sunk costs is that we become riveted to the past. We become obsessed with what was rather than seeing and acting upon what now is. For instance, if you buy shares at £10 each and the price falls to 80p, you may be unwilling to sell for less than £10 because, as you see it, that is the 'correct' price. In other words, the £10 invested becomes the reference point for subsequent decisions.

Researchers who studied bidding prices on the internet auction site eBay discovered something interesting. They wanted to know whether setting a reserve price is a good idea. By analysing large amounts of information, they discovered that sellers who dispensed with reserve prices and who started from very low bids tended to achieve higher prices than those who imposed a reserve price. The researchers inferred from their results that starting low without a reserve price creates a 'sunk cost' effect as frequent bidding involves investing time and effort. Consequently, as the price of an item rises, early bidders may be reluctant to forgo their sunk costs and therefore become determined to acquire the item at all costs. (The risk with this strategy of course is that if there are few bidders, you may have to sell a valuable item cheap!)

The eBay research also suggests that it is not just money that counts. We may become psychologically attached to the time and the physical and emotional effort invested. This is Brian's problem. Brian owns a business that makes very little money. Financially he knows he would be better off closing it down and finding alternative employment. Emotionally he cannot bring himself to do it because of all that he has invested in the business over the years. He says:

> What's holding me here is not being able to let go of the nearly £200,000 that I've put into it [the business]. It's very difficult to say goodbye to that – although I know it's gone. Because it's just not your money; you've put your heart and soul into it.

In contrast, when Sabina's business began losing money she did the right thing. She said, 'I've got jackets which I bought for twenty pound. I'm selling them for three pound... It's hard, it's very, very hard.'

Hard though it was for Sabina to sell substantially below cost, it is the correct decision from an economic standpoint because it means she can at least salvage something from an unhappy situation. She can use the money to buy new stock that might sell better than the jackets, and can clear space and start again, unlike Brian, who remains shackled by the past. Research has shown, however, that entrepreneurs are more likely to keep businesses they have started themselves even if they are unprofitable, and sell businesses that they have bought, even if they are outperforming the businesses they have started!

It is not difficult to see why entrepreneurs make such decisions. Starting a business involves expending much more time and effort than simply buying a going concern, so the sunk costs are much higher. Economically, however, it is like climbing up an apple tree and ignoring the windfalls.

GOLDEN RULE

The golden rule when making decisions involving sunk costs is to focus upon achieving the best possible return on investment for the future. This means seeing the situation not for what it was but for what it has become. What you paid for shares is irrelevant. If the price falls, the reality is that you have 80p multiplied by the number of shares to invest. The question is whether those remaining funds could be invested more profitably elsewhere.

Base decisions on best returns for the future.

Alan's friend persuaded him to invest £70,000 (half of his retirement lump sum) in a business venture. The venture failed and Alan's friend then said that his only hope of recouping his £70,000 was to reinvest the remainder of his lump sum in the business. What would you do if you were Alan?

Alan did as the friend suggested and ended up losing another £70,000. Financially unsophisticated, Alan was unaware that his friend was manipulating 'sunk costs' by emphasizing the lost £70,000, when the economically wise and ethically proper question was whether Alan should take such a huge risk with the remainder of his funds. Given the importance of those funds to Alan, the answer surely had to be 'no'.

WASTE NOT, WANT NOT?

Imagine choosing between two 'TV' dinners. The dinners are identical and they both have the same 'eat by' date. The only difference is that one cost £7.99 and the other was bought on a special offer for £4.99. Which of the two dinners would you choose?

Logically it makes no difference, but when researchers conducted the experiment they discovered that a significant proportion of diners selected the more expensive meal. We can infer from those results that as human beings we dislike waste. While waste may be morally abhorrent, our abhorrence can sometimes lead to poor decisions. For instance, research has shown that the more we pay for a theatre ticket, the more likely we are to use it. Yet if it is a poor production, persistence only makes matters worst. Having spent money on the tickets, you then end up paying to travel into town, paying parking costs and, to cap it all, waste an evening. The correct question is: what else could you do with the time and money?

Theatre tickets and wasted evenings are one thing. Supposing, however, the decision involves buying a bulk consignment of stock. Some of the items in consignment are unusable and will therefore be wasted. Would you rather take the more expensive option of buying singly? Don't be afraid to 'waste' something if it makes economic sense to do so.

SUNK COSTS AND SUCCESS

The sunk costs rule also applies to successful decisions. All else equal, if an opportunity offering a better return upon investment becomes available, we should take it *even though* it means abandoning a successful course of action.

Anne was lucky. She applied for two jobs and got both. The first job involved attending a two-day assessment centre, sitting a battery of tests and undergoing two searching interviews. It pays £25,000 a year. The second job involved only a 40-minute interview that was really little more than a pleasant chat over tea and biscuits. It pays £35,000 a year. Anne feels that having worked so hard for the first job, she ought to take it. Since, however, all that effort has no bearing on what happens next, all else being equal Anne should reject the first job because the second one offers the best return for the *future*.

THE PAST

Few of us in the Western world will ever experience the devastation that war and natural disasters can create. Survivors are left with nothing for it but to rebuild their lives as best they can, sometimes having lost literally everything: their home, their livelihood and their family. Fortunes can be transformed within seconds. The time it takes for a tidal wave to wash in represents the division between the past and the future. What was maybe only a few seconds ago, no longer is.

The past is dust.

What is past is past. We cannot recall the past five minutes, never mind the past five years. The sooner we recognize this, the better, for if we cling to the past we risk losing what the future might offer.

Pursue the unattainable and lose the possible.

Fergus had been a fisherman all his life, as had his father and his father before him. When the fishing industry declined, Fergus promptly accepted the inevitable and converted his fishing boat to take passengers. It was a hard decision because his whole life was invested in the fishing industry. Yet Fergus is glad that he made the decision, as he now enjoys a second career operating educational and pleasure cruises around the harbour. If Fergus had buried his head in the sand and clung to fishing, he would have gradually gone bankrupt. Then he would have had no money to convert his boat. Besides, someone else might have beaten him to the new business opportunity.

The principle also applies to day-to-day decisions. It is always disappointing when a customer walks away, particularly if you have invested a lot of time and effort trying to achieve a sale. If that happens, respond with charm. Hand the customer your business card and wish them well. Today's sale is lost but there is always a tomorrow.

COUNT THE COST

Easier said than done, you might say. One way of reducing the emotional pain of letting go is to reframe the issue. That is, rather than thinking only of the cost of letting go, consider the cost of persistence.

The real cost of anything is what you could have had instead.

Recall, our hypothetical shopkeeper could earn £2.86 per hour as a shop-keeper or £8.75 an hour stocking shelves in the supermarket. In other words, keeping the shop costs him or her £5.89 an hour. Expressing the issue as a loss encourages us to think about whether persistence is a price worth paying, and if so, why?

EXCEPTIONS TO THE RULE

Sometimes it is wise to persist despite setbacks. More specifically, persistence may be economically wise if:

- the likely pay-off is high; and
- the project is almost complete.

Peter wanted to be a surveyor. His long-term goal was to found a commercial property practice. He invested thousands of pounds in fees and living expenses in order to qualify. Peter worked hard at the course but his mother died shortly before the examinations so he missed one exam. It meant that a year had to elapse before Peter could resit the exam.

Unable to find work in a surveyor's office, Peter took a clerical job in the public relations department of a multinational electronics firm. Two things then happened that were completely unexpected. First, Peter discovered that he liked working in public relations. Second, the firm offered to sponsor him for an MBA.

Naturally, Peter was in a quandary about whether he should accept the offer or become a surveyor as planned. There was a compounding factor. Peter found commercial property work boring but enjoyed boundary disputes, arbitration and the like. The problem for Peter is that this kind of work is relatively hard to come by, and the pay compares poorly with that for work concerned with commercial property.

What should Peter do? Abandon his chosen profession and write off the expense? Alternatively, grit his teeth and endure the boredom of his chosen path? Or compromise and start a general street practice?

Peter's first task is to complete the course, because additional investment can affect the future. Moreover, the course is over 90 per cent complete. The amount of additional time and effort required to qualify is minuscule and the prospective pay-off is high. Notice that I did *not* say that Peter should become a surveyor. I merely suggested that he should invest just a little more in order to complete the course. The investment is justified because completion buys Peter an option that he can always exercise later. We discuss in Chapter 10 how options can be used to manage uncertainty. Here we need only note that options can be used to create launch pads for future possibilities.

This still leaves the question of what Peter should do next. The possibilities include:

- becoming a commercial property surveyor, possibly well off but definitely miserable;
- specializing in resolving legal disputes, relatively poor but happy;
- being a successful PR executive, quite well off and happy.

Of course Peter might find that practising as a commercial property surveyor is more interesting than studying to be one. That still leaves the problem of how to decide. Representing clients in legal disputes and public relations may seem poles apart but Peter may find them both attractive because both require an extrovert (even exhibitionist) streak. Moreover, the company must have been impressed with Peter's performance to want to invest in him. That in itself is highly significant.

It is also important to separate means from ends. Assuming that interesting work and money are equally important to Peter, a simple even swap analysis (see Chapter 3) will show that option 3 is the optimal choice because it enables him to achieve both of his important goals. Moreover, it does not preclude the possibility of business ownership, as Peter could eventually start his own public relations consultancy.

DOLLARS, SENSE AND SUNK COSTS

What do you do if you have started converting an old mill to flats and the property market crashes? The heading of this section is actually the title of an influential academic paper by Gregory Northcraft and Gerrit Wolf, who argue that some projects can absorb a certain amount of failure; that is, where there is a gap between intended and realized costs and revenues. In a nutshell, the earlier in the projects life costs are incurred and the later in a project that revenues begin to flow, the greater will be the so-called region of rationality whereby setbacks can be absorbed.

For example, few so-called long haul projects such as building bridges or digging tunnels are ever completed on time and to budget, but they are nevertheless worth completing despite cost overruns because of likely revenues.

Table 4.1

1 High pay-off: low completion *Questionable*	2 High pay-off: completion close *Worth persisting*
3 Low pay-off: low completion *Abandon*	4 Completion close: pay-off low *Questionable*

You can use this simple table to structure your thinking about sunk costs and whether something is worth completing. The easiest decisions to make concern projects in square 3, where little has been invested and the likely pay-off is extremely modest. Such ventures are probably best abandoned. Decisions concerning projects in square 2 are also relatively easy. If a project is almost finished and the likely pay-off is high, it is probably sensible to persist with it. For example, if you were building a toll bridge and needed just another bucket of cement to finish the job, you would hardly abandon the venture given the revenues that you would be about to recoup!

The trouble is, not all decisions are as clear-cut as this. The most difficult decisions to make concern projects falling into either square 1 or square 4, as the answer is that 'it all depends'. In square 1 – high pay-off, low completion – it might depend upon precisely what is meant by those terms and what the alternatives are. Again, for decisions in square 4 – low reward, high completion – 'it all depends' on the circumstances. For instance, companies sometimes market products that have not lived up to promises made at the research and development stage, or have been overtaken by competitors swifter to market. The rationale is that having invested millions in these second-rate satellite navigation systems, mobile phones, MP3 players and the like, they might as well try to recoup their outlay as best they can. Whether 'recovery through use' is wise depends upon whether the additional resources needed to finally get the product to market, and the resources needed to subsequently support it, could be spent on more profitable products.

Calculating whether persistence is worthwhile is a specialist task beyond the scope of this book. You would be well advised to consult an accountant to estimate what cost overruns and/or revenue shortfalls the project can absorb — known as the 'region of rationality'.

NONSENSE AND SUNK COSTS

In order to estimate cost overruns, the accountant will need to know how close the project is to completion. Beware! Psychologists have discovered that the answer to the question is likely to be unconsciously biased.

The more we have invested, the more optimistic we become.

An interesting experiment involved asking two groups of students to read a scenario about a project to build a new type of plane that cannot be detected by radar. The two groups were asked to estimate how certain they were that the project would succeed: 80 per cent certain, 90 per cent certain and so forth. Group 1 learned that project was at an early stage and very little money had been invested. The second group was told that construction was already under way and that millions of dollars had already been invested. The second group were much more optimistic about the chances of success!

WHEN YOU SHOULD BREAK THE BANK

Using budgets to control expenditure and minimize the risk of runaway projects (see Chapter 10) is wise — but with one proviso. Never halt a project just because the budget is spent. This is because budget depletion constitutes what accountants call a non-informative loss. In other words, it merely tells you that a certain amount of money has been expended to date. It says nothing about the state of the project and whether it is worth completing.

Research has shown, moreover, that budgeting can lead to decisions that are economically unwise. More specifically, evidence suggests that entrepreneurs tend to be more reluctant to allocate more resources if the budget has already been spent than if a portion of it remains. Indeed, we hear it often enough in big organizations that X and Y are proscribed because 'there is no money in the budget'. One of the joys of being an entrepreneur is that you have the freedom and competitive advantage of being able to channel resources into the most promising directions without first needing to appeal to any number of committees. Don't be afraid to use it.

TIME VERSUS MONEY

We may be more inclined to invest time to salvage lost money than invest more money, or vice versa.

Money you can replace.
Time is gone for ever.

Be careful! The slogan 'time equals risk' should remind us that while quick fixes based upon an injection of cash may be defensible, we should be wary of extending timetables, as we may discover that by the time the venture is complete, it has been overtaken by events. In 1993 the London Stock Exchange abandoned project TAURUS, an IT-based venture designed to facilitate electronic settlement of stocks and shares. The Stock Exchange had spent over £80 million on the venture, and banks and investment houses an estimated £400 million (1993 figures). Even so, 18 months into construction they decided to cancel the project and start again. It was not the money that was the deciding factor but the time. The then chief executive, Peter Rawlins, hammered out his message to the board:

> Of course we can carry on if you are prepared to vote the money, but I am telling you the issue is not the money. It is the time... The only way to go forward now is [that]... we say, 'Stop! Spend not one further penny.' The Stock Exchange is going to finish building the central infrastructure... It is going to be fifteen months... In the meantime, all you guys out there stand down your entire teams with no certain knowledge as to what you have still got to do. Are you going to vote for that?[1]

It is a matter of record that the board did not vote for this option. More recently, the UK National Health Service's electronic patient record system has fallen so far behind schedule that it seems destined either never to appear or, if it is ever completed, to have been overtaken by events.

Losing money is bad enough but money can be replaced. Energy too can be replenished. In contrast, a moment of elapsed time is gone for ever. In thinking about whether or not to discontinue a venture, consider the value of your own time. Significantly, advertisements for Breitling watches carry the slogan 'Time: our greatest luxury'. The dying Queen Elizabeth I of England made the point more directly: 'All my riches for a moment of time.'

Summary

1. Sunk costs should normally be ignored when deciding how to invest resources.

2. The correct approach is to select the option that promises maximum return upon investment for the future.

3. This may actually mean dropping a successful decision.

4. If it is emotionally difficult to forgo past investments, calculate what persistence is costing you.

5. Where large and complex projects are involved, seek professional help in determining whether and to what extent persistence makes economic sense.

6. Try not to deceive yourself about the state of a project.

7. Don't let budgets hold you back.

8. Time equals risk.

9. Money and energy can be replenished; never time.

NOTES

1. Cited in Drummond, H (1996) *Escalation in Decision-Making: The Tragedy of Taurus*, Oxford University Press, Oxford, p 151

5

Black Swans

– decision making under stress

Not till you abandon all thoughts of seeking something will you be on the right road.

(Zen proverb)

 **Key message:** Take charge

Running for the rents, running for the rates for wages and staff... you won't believe it... I've got income tax, I've got VAT to pay, I've got [an] accountant to pay. Where is that money going to come? It's hard. It's very, very hard.

(An entrepreneur)

Just before Christmas I sold a dress to somebody. I sold it for £40. It was a Christmas dress. She had broken it. All the crystals have all come out. She had washed it. She said even the label wasn't inside and all the dresses have got labels inside with washing instructions – she want [sic] a refund!

(An entrepreneur)

The entrepreneur's metaphorical kitchen is hot: anxiety about getting paid, customers complaining, the government forever introducing new laws to make business more difficult and more expensive. There are ominous envelopes from the Inland Revenue awaiting your attention. Partners may not be pulling their weight – and so on.

To a point, stress is probably what you enjoy. But only to a point! Too much stress is destructive. Even moderate levels of stress can undermine decision-making ability, while prolonged stress can result in serious illness and even early death. This chapter explains what causes stress and what entrepreneurs can do to reduce stress, while simultaneously improving the performance and profitability of the firm.

WHAT IS STRESS?

The word 'stress' derives from the Latin word stringer, meaning to draw tight. The concept of stress emanates from physics and engineering, where pressure is seen as resulting in strain and ultimately fracture – hence, for example, 'nervous breakdown' or 'the straw that broke the camel's back'. Psychologists regard stress as

> a person's *adaptive* response to any form of stimulus that places *excessive* psychological or physical *demands* upon them.

A stressor is any psychological or physical factor that places excessive demand upon the individual. It can be virtually anything: a sudden loud noise, an interruption, a piece of equipment failing, through to the more chronic forms of stress such as long hours and constant long-distance travel.

To be more precise, stress results from the gap between:

▮ the demands placed upon the individual; and
▮ the individual's ability to cope with those demands.

The bigger and more uncontrollable the gap between demands made and coping ability, the higher the level of the stress experienced by the individual.

Note that the individual must experience the demand as excessive and uncontrollable for it to be stressful. Moreover, stress only results where the demand threatens something important to the individual. This explains why different people find different things stressful, though, as we shall see later, there are things that stress most people.

STRESS PATTERNS

People typically respond to excessive demands in three stages:

1. alarm;
2. resistance;
3. exhaustion.

Stage 1 occurs when an individual encounters a stressor. Metaphorically speaking, an *alarm* bell rings, such as 'I'll never finish this job on time.' The stressor then presents the individual with a choice between coping with the situation or avoiding it, known as 'fight or flight'.

The second stage, *resistance*, occurs when the person decides to try to cope with the situation. For example, the person may brew a strong cup of coffee in an attempt to revive their energies, or may forgo a lunch break or decide to work late.

Sometimes the individual succeeds in meeting the demands placed upon them. Prolonged and repeated exposure to stress can lead to *exhaustion*, however, as the individual's ability to cope crumbles.

Another way of conceptualizing stress is as a mismatch between the individual and their environment. Individuals, it is suggested, attempt to maintain a stable relationship between their thoughts, emotions and their environment. In this view, individuals may be seen as possessing a 'range of stability' within which they can cope fairly comfortably with the physical and emotional demands of their environment. A stressor is any factor that drives individuals beyond their 'range of stability', forcing them to respond in order to restore stability. This is known as the adjustment process or coping strategy. However we conceptualize it, the end result of prolonged exposure to stress is the same; that is, exhaustion.

WHY IS STRESS HARMFUL?

Prolonged exposure to stress is associated with a long list of illnesses. Although the precise links between stress and illness are unclear, medical scientists believe that stress probably damages the body's immune system, rather as does the AIDS virus, thus leaving the person vulnerable to life-threatening illnesses including coronary thrombosis (heart attack) and strokes, and less serious but nevertheless debilitating conditions such as headaches, ulcers and insomnia. Stress is also associated with profound psychological problems including anxiety and depression, and can undermine our ability to manage our business and make good decisions.

A vicious circle may be set in train whereby people experiencing stress damage their health by resorting to excessive smoking or excessive alcohol consumption. Such behaviours afford temporary relief but at the expense of compounding the stress, thus triggering more damaging coping behaviours.

WHAT CAUSES STRESS?

There are seven general causes of stress:

1. overload;
2. underload;
3. responsibility for others;
4. personality and demands for success;
5. relationships with others;
6. major life changes;
7. daily interruptions and problems.

Overload arises from either having too much to do, or undertaking tasks that are too difficult. For instance, in the early years you may be busy running the business all day, travelling here and there, spending every evening doing paperwork and every weekend visiting trade fairs, buying stock, transporting equipment and materials and so forth. Even as the business matures, the responsibility for it is constant – '24/7'. In addition, there are almost always new demands, such as implementing health and safety regulations, wrestling with software problems, keeping abreast of new technology, to name but a few.

Having too little to do is as bad as (and sometimes worse than) having too much to do. **Underload** too can be either quantitative or qualitative. For example, if trade drops during the summer months, you may be underemployed. If you are unable to afford staff, you may become burdened with unstimulating chores. A butcher who fell on hard times describes his disgust at being obliged to sell pigs' feet:

... five pigs' feet for a £1. Then you've got to chop 'em into small pieces, cut the toenails off of them, put them in a carrier bag which costs 5p and then they'll [customers] ask you for another carrier bag − by then your arm is aching − bloody pigs' feet! Cutting pigs' feet in the winter and pork bones. Oh my God! If somebody would have told me that I would have been selling pigs' feet and pork bones 10 years ago I'd have said, 'Never in a month of Sundays! Never!'

Recall that stress results from the uncontrollable demands that are made upon us. People are the biggest source of variation in a business, so it is hardly surprising that responsibility for others is stressful. *You* may be highly committed to the success of the business, but your employees may not always share your enthusiasm. Martin describes his exasperation with an under-enthusiastic employee:

She was supposed to start at nine but she called off at the supermarket for a bottle of water so it was always five past nine before she arrived. Then, because of all this water, she was always going to the loo [toilet]. So, I wasn't only losing money on her work, it was costing me a fortune because she used so much bloody water. She went to the toilet so often you could deduce when she left from my water bills... And the amount of toilet paper she used... Instead of saying, 'What is all this about?', you let it go until you are actually noticing toilet paper.

That was only the start, however. Martin tried to discuss his concerns with the employee:

We had a couple of talks... I said, 'I am under the impression that you come to work with the attitude of "I will do as little as possible"... You are a first-class skiver [work-shy]. You are no good to me.'

Admonishment made no difference. Eventually Martin produced timesheets that consistently showed a maximum of four hours' input for an eight-hour day. The employee was unmoved, however:

She said, 'Well, I can't drag them [customers] off the streets, can I?' I said, 'No, but when they do come in you could leap up a bit and be a bit more excited... give them a card with your name on it and say you look forward to seeing them again.'
She said, 'Oh, I don't agree with all that.'

Then there was Alan. Alan had a customer who placed a large order. 'And do you know what,' said Alan, 'I was rude to him!' Being rude to your best customer suggests severe stress. Significantly, Alan was facing a tax investigation at the time – a form of overload. The investigation dragged on for three years, plunging Alan into depression. Eventually he was exonerated and the Inland Revenue cancelled an outstanding debt in recognition of the unreasonable timescale. By then, of course, the damage was done.

Entrepreneurs frequently resemble what psychologists call 'Type A' **personalities**. Type A's are particularly stress prone because they are ambitious, demanding, results orientated, impatient and driven – sometimes to the point of an obsessive and compulsive **need for achievement and success**. Yet the pleasure obtained from success is only a fraction of the pain created by failure. In August 2008, multi-millionaire businessman Christopher Foster shot his wife, his daughter and his collection of animals before setting fire to his home and shooting himself – an act believed to have been precipitated by the imminent collapse of his business empire.

Foster's is an extreme case. Some entrepreneurs content themselves with committing psychological suicide. When Bob's business failed, he retreated to the settee and devoted his days to drinking cans of beer, throwing the empties into the corner of his living room. Another entrepreneur said:

> When you've worked for yourself, you would like to see something for those 25 years – because that's why you've worked 70-odd hours a week. You're always working for the future. You're always working for tomorrow. And you get to your mid-forties and you think, 'Well, hang on a minute, when does this future arrive?' You seem to be putting it off and putting it off. At some time in your life you've got to take stock and think to yourself, 'Well, the future's got to be here – sooner or later.'

'**Major life transitions**' refers to the big events in our lives. The loss of a spouse registers 100 on the scale of stressful impact. Divorce or separation is next on the list, along with major illness, both registering 50 points. In business, the experience of merging or demerging, or of being involved in a takeover bid, or experiencing the loss of a major customer are major transitions.

Major life transitions are stressful because of the scale of adjustment required. Misfortune loves company, so one major change like divorce can trigger a series of other changes such as loss of one's home and children, loss of financial security – all adding to the stress. This was Peter's experience when divorce coincided with a business downturn:

The business is my life, as a marriage is to most people. Sometimes I feel I have lost everything. I've lost my family, I've lost my children because I don't see them and [in tears] I may very well be losing the business in the near future.

Peter's problems were so acute that he decided that he could not afford £70 to replace a broken security camera: 'I might need that money for something else,' he said.

Interestingly, good experiences such as winning a large sum of money, achieving a major contract or completing a successful acquisition can also be stressful, as they too require adjustment. Many entrepreneurs find retirement more stressful than working because the transition from a full and busy life to a sedentary existence does not suit their restless nature.

Entrepreneurs are exposed to the same **daily interruptions and problems** as the rest of us. The central heating boiler fails; the children get mumps; the dog gets into a fight and has to be taken to the vet; the invoice arrives but not the goods. These minor problems are stressful because they throw us off our game plan and disrupt other important activities. Indeed, psychologists believe they may actually be more stressful than the seemingly much bigger problems posed by major life transitions.

ANXIETY AND DEPRESSION

Anxiety and depression are close cousins of stress. Neither mind-state is conducive to sound decision making. Anxious individuals tend to have a greater need to justify decisions than non-anxious people and are therefore thought to be more susceptible to the social pressure associated with escalation (see Chapter 10). Anxious people tend to be hyper-vigilant and may therefore see threats where none exist, thus adding to the stress load. Anxiety can also produce what psychologists call 'threat rigidity'. More specifically, the rationally correct response to a perceived threat is to broaden one's information so as to create a more accurate and comprehensive picture. Anxiety blocks the ability to do this. Anxious individuals typically narrow down their information. Moreover, instead of changing ineffective practices and routines, anxious individuals tend to follow them more rigidly. Peter's behaviour is consistent with 'threat rigidity'. Rather than spend £70 on a new security camera, he made his life even more stressful by trying to keep watch himself. In the end, he lost a lot more money than £70 through pilfering.

Whereas anxiety results in a tendency towards over-control, depression is thought to have the opposite effect. Depressed people typically perceive that they have little or no control over events and therefore conclude that there is nothing they can do to improve their situation, because they fail to see any link between their actions and the outcomes of those actions.

Depressed people can suffer because they systematically underestimate their chances of success relative to people who are not depressed. As Peter emerged from the trauma of separation and divorce, he cashed in on government funding to regenerate the business. That important opportunity had been there all along, staring Peter in the face in fact, but it took him almost three years to act, because in his depressed state he temporarily lost faith in his ability to succeed. Yet had he pursued that opportunity three years earlier, he could have saved himself much anxiety and misery.

Depression damages the ability of the body's immune system to protect itself against pathogenic processes that cause illness and disease. It is unclear whether altered immune function is caused by depression as such, or by problems that typically accompany depression such as disrupted sleep patterns, poor appetite and increased alcohol consumption. One theory suggests that depression results from exposure to uncontrollable stressors. Another possibility is that depression is itself a stressor. What is clear, however, is that depressed people are more susceptible to illness, and more likely to have an accident and/or endanger others than people who are not depressed. (Incidentally, if you have an employee who is suffering from depression, be very careful about what work you allow him or her to do.) Depression may also be a defensive mechanism against extreme stress, nature's way of slowing us down. Nothing goes on getting better indefinitely and so peak performance can shade into depression. Indeed, there may be a fine line between the two.

TAKING CHARGE

Stressful events frequently represent 'black swans'. Europeans believed that all swans were white until explorers discovered Australia. Black swans thus signify the unexpected – the uncontrollable factors that produce additional stress. Taking charge is the antidote.

Taking charge means recognizing that stress is partly self-inflicted. Christopher Foster's suicide was triggered by a decision to dishonour a contract. The company concerned sued, and from that point his fortunes declined rapidly. The point is that Foster *chose* to dishonour the contract, just as other entrepreneurs choose to mount takeover bids, choose to launch new products and so forth. If the metaphorical kitchen is already too hot, why turn up the temperature? What do you hope to gain?

STRESS BUSTER 1: THE 80/20 RULE

Although black swans are by definition unpredictable, you can be fairly certain that something untoward will happen even if you cannot be specific. Prepare for the unexpected by holding resources – material and mental – in reserve. The so-called 80/20 ratio is a useful guide here. That is, avoid committing more than 80 per cent so that you have a margin to cater for eventualities. For example, when scheduling projects or even just planning your daily time schedule, leave a 20 per cent safety margin so that you can respond to unforeseen demands.

Expect the unexpected.

Reserves will not eliminate 'black swans', but they reduce problems of overload and leave you less stressed as a result. They will also enable you to seize opportunities; that is, the good 'black swans' that suddenly appear and that you might otherwise not have time for.

STRESS BUSTER 2: STOP SHORT OF PERFECTION

The most common form of overload is taking too much on. It is better to start one project and finish it than to become involved in six and deliver nothing.

It is also a question of what you deliver. Perfection is expensive. When building a battleship, getting 80 per cent of functionality right is relatively cheap and easy. It is the remaining 20 per cent – that is, adding the refinements, the so-called bells and whistles – that ramps up cost and results in projects falling behind schedule. Do you need to be so ambitious? For instance, if you are a travel agent, is it better to sell 80 per cent of seats on two chartered flights than exert maximum effort to sell 100 per cent of seats on one flight, only for the other plane to leave less than half full because of your preoccupation with the former? When it comes to collecting debts, the chances are that 80 per cent of the amount owing results from a few very large bad debts. Pursue the 'big fish' first rather than waste energy on the umpteen 'minnows' that constitute the other 20 per cent of the total.

STRESS BUSTER 3: GET ORGANIZED

A poorly organized business falls into a vicious circle. Poor organization creates more work and loses money – which then creates more stress. In contrast, a well-run business creates the opposite dynamic of a virtuous circle.

Work smart as well as hard.

One reason why Bill Gates has made a lot more money than many other contemporary high-profile entrepreneurs is his insistence upon careful planning, coupled with a determination to generate 'bottom line' results. You can do the same. Start by installing systems to promote the effective running of the business. For example, make sure that invoices are dispatched promptly, use a diary system whereby non-payers and other unresolved issues are brought to your attention regularly, and ensure that staff know the procedures to be followed and standards expected of them. It takes time, but it yields rewards. It is rather like Robinson Crusoe, who could never improve his desert island home because he was always fishing for food. One day he went hungry and made a net.

Maintaining a database of customers on a computer or manual log rather than in your head saves time rummaging for information. Good systems also mean that you can delegate more. Besides, you can use the database to generate more turnover and profit from the business by anticipating customers' needs. For example, you can use a simple computer-based diary system to remind you to telephone for orders rather than wait passively for customers to come to you. Being proactive reduces the likelihood of customer migration. Generating repeat business is a lot cheaper than advertising for new customers. Installing systems like 'total quality management' costs money and demands effort in the short run. In the long run, however, the resultant efficiency gains are likely to be well worth it. In addition, accreditation may mean that you are eligible to bid for a wider range of contracts and can raise your prices.

Periodically review what an hour of your time is worth. Of course you know how to use Microsoft Word, but does it makes sense for you to sit typing letters any more? Ask yourself whether the time could be better spent perhaps visiting trade fairs, calling upon customers, thinking of new ideas for business and so on. Think hard about what you can delegate. In all, it is the difference between working hard and working smart.

Impose order before there is disorder.

Be proactive about garnering the harvest. One of the biggest sources of stress in business is worrying about getting paid. Good systems will help, but don't wait passively for the cheque to arrive. Statements, telephone calls and even making an unexpected visit to laggards will ensure that your invoice is at the top of the pile when payments are made. Better still, make it your ambition to work for the day when you can afford to decline offers of business from habitual non-payers and aggressive customers.

'A stitch in time saves nine,' counsels the proverb. Inevitably things go wrong, even in the best-run organizations. Since problems have a habit of compounding exponentially, it is wise to deal with them while they are small and containable – well before you start noticing toilet paper, that is.

Fix small problems promptly.

Resist any temptation to procrastinate. For example, if you see an employee engaging in a potentially dangerous working practice, intervene before someone is killed or seriously injured. If materials from a new supplier are wreaking havoc with quality, do not let the problem escalate by turning out substandard items; stop production. If a window is broken, ensure that it is repaired promptly. Telephoning a joiner is a lot less stressful than mopping up after a flood.

STRESS BUSTER 4: DEFY TIME

Stress is sometimes referred to as the 'black plague' of the 20th century. Significantly, the advent of the 'black plague' coincided with the emergence of the clock as the foremost means of regulating our lives. Our days are punctuated by starting times, finishing times, mealtimes, break time and so forth. Just about every electrical gadget we own incorporates a clock. Yet there was a time when time counted for nothing. The agricultural peasant rose when it was light and slept when it was dark. There was no division of time between work and leisure. Time only became important after the Industrial Revolution and the emergence of the factory system, which needed synchronization.

Clock time now seems so important that we almost always respond to pressure by speeding up. This is what stress loves! Instead of going faster and becoming more stressed as a result – 'more haste, less speed' – try going as slowly as you possibly can. Going slow, taking your time, is a subtle way of taking charge. Instead of being ruled by deadlines and rushing to meet targets, proceed at your own pace.

Go slow to go fast.

Interestingly, when something becomes not a matter of time, it is often finished surprisingly quickly.

STRESS BUSTER 5: PRIORITIZE

Black swans may not arrive singly, so overload cannot always be avoided. Students of the martial arts practise routines that simulate an attack by multiple assailants. They learn to deal with the assailant who is closest first, precisely because this assailant's physical proximity means that he or she is best positioned to inflict damage.

This maxim works well for managing overload.

First things first.

If you are under pressure, begin by compiling a list of everything you need to do. Highlight the more urgent tasks and then prioritize the shortlist. Start with the most urgent task and then move through the others.

STRESS BUSTER 6: REBOOT

Just as a clockwork toy eventually loses momentum, a business can lose energy and direction over time. If the business seems to be going through a bad patch, try the following simple health check:

1. Who are my customers?
2. What do they want?
3. What are they willing to pay for?
4. Has any of this changed?

The aim of the exercise is to detect possible slippage between what your customers value and what you are actually delivering. For instance, Toyota's customers value reliability. Caterpillar attracts custom by its exemplary after-sales service. Hospitals in developing countries create value by treating patients at the lowest possible costs. In contrast, in affluent countries cost is less important in health care than using the latest and best treatments, for which hospitals charge a price premium. Likewise, architectural firms may create value by focusing upon low-cost housing solutions or specializing in upmarket residential properties, according to what particular segment of the market they are in. Is the business still sharply aligned to what your customers value, or have things slipped a little?

Slippage means loss of efficiency. Resources need to be organized and reorganized to deliver value. Companies such as Microsoft and Google would never have succeeded if they had merely employed scientists and computer engineers and just left them to get on with the job. All systems decay. It is necessary, periodically, to review and if necessary redesign systems and to redirect knowledge, expertise and so forth to match what customers value. For example, this might involve installing new office software, selling off parts of the business that are a poor fit with the core enterprise, or improving quality so that customer expectations are again fulfilled.

STRESS BUSTER 7: REFRESH

Imagine a knife that gets used day in, day out. Eventually the blade becomes blunt. If we carry on using the knife, we end up exerting more and more effort for ever-diminishing returns. Breaks, holidays, travelling to conferences and so forth should be seen not as luxuries but as normal business expenses essential to maintaining long-term capability. You replace toner in the photocopier and top up the oil in a car, so why not refresh and recharge yourself?

STRESS BUSTER 8: MANAGE EXPECTATIONS

Depression equals the gap between our expectations and our achievements. Ignore the popular books promising instant wealth, and the self-serving autobiographies of entrepreneurs trumpeting effortless success. Unless you are miraculously lucky, those promises merely create false expectations.

Divide and conquer.

Set expectations that are measurable. Dreamlike hopes, like 'waiting for that day', are almost bound to produce depression because they are so vague that they can never be achieved. If you do not know what success looks like, how can you hope to recognize it?

Be specific about what counts as success; for example:

- increasing turnover by 10 per cent every year for the next five years;
- acquiring one new customer every day/week/month (as appropriate);
- buying a country residence within three years.

Be ambitious about what you want to achieve but realistic as to how you will get there. Translate the larger, more distant goal into smaller, easily attainable targets. That way, instead of feeling that you are forever working hard to reach a seemingly impossible goal, you will generate a constant stream of progress and a constant boost to your self-esteem. Self-esteem matters, because research by psychologists has consistently shown that individuals with high self-esteem tend to be more successful than individuals with low self-esteem – hence the proverb 'nothing succeeds like success.' If that seems to contradict the advice given in Chapter 2, it is only when you are consistently successful that success can become a liability. Worry about that later; it is a nice problem to have!

Review the plan periodically. Planning is basically dreaming with discipline. You may never achieve all or even anything on the plan and yet still be enormously successful through taking unplanned and unforeseen opportunities. Remember: black swans can be a Good Thing!

Be prepared to adjust the plan if circumstances dictate. Misery is inevitable if you retain unrealistic targets such as trying to increase turnover in a falling market. Instead, lower the threshold temporarily. For instance, Paul had been very successful over the years until the economic cycle turned against him. Yet he kept setting targets that were no longer feasible, and became depressed when he failed to achieve them. 'The trade wasn't there any more,' said Paul. 'But I couldn't see it.'

Incidentally, success may not follow a linear trajectory. It can come in fits and starts with long periods of dearth. You may have one very successful project that pays for nine other failures. It is not failure per se that produces depression, but expectation that everything should succeed.

STRESS BUSTER 9: REINVENT YOURSELF

Nothing lasts for ever. Stepping down from day-to-day control of the business is a major life transition. That does not mean you have to give up, however. One option is to do the same thing rescored in a different key. In 2008, Bill Gates stepped down from Microsoft in order to concentrate upon his charitable foundation. Gates exchanged a life of fighting lawsuits and strategic battles to stay afloat amid rapidly changing technology for one spent contending with diseases such as AIDS and malaria.

Go with the flow.

Alternatively, instead of changing what you do, change how you do it. For the past 35 years I have stayed at an old inn. The landlady is now in her eighties and day-to-day management of the inn has long since passed to younger members of the family. Yet she still awakens to the 7 o'clock news on Radio 4, dons an apron and is in the kitchen by 8 o'clock. She clears a plate or two from a breakfasting guest before sitting down with the family to breakfast. She is also dressed up and present at the start of lunch and early evening, when she chats to regulars and again removes a plate or two. The result is happiness and fulfilment. The landlady still feels she is doing productive work (and she is), but is doing so at a pace that matches her abilities. It is the difference between going with the flow and going against it.

STRESS BUSTER 10: CULTIVATE TRANQUILLITY

Try to avoid making important decisions when stressed. Research by psychologists has shown that we are much more likely to see solutions to problems when we approach them in a relaxed state of mind than when feeling tense or tired. If that is impractical, make allowances for how you feel. If you are feeling anxious, revise your estimates of success downwards. If you are feeling depressed, scale them up.

An empty mind is a powerful mind.

Better still, try to get yourself into a frame of mind conducive to good decision making. Frame of mind cannot be forced but it can be coaxed. Exercise is an excellent stress buster. So is meditation. Instead of filling your mind with all the problems of the day, try emptying it. I practise this philosophy by listening to Radio 3 in the morning. (And no matter how busy I am, or how early I have to rise, the day does not begin until I have consumed a pot of coffee.) I have heard many people say that Choral Evensong (also broadcast on Radio 3) has a soothing effect regardless of one's religious beliefs or non-beliefs.

Draw a distinction between signal and noise. What was worrying you this time last year and how important is it now? Most of what bombards us is noise. That is why there is not much of a market for old newspapers. Some decision makers carry works by Virgil or St Augustine in their pockets to rebalance their perennial preoccupation with the here and now.

ULTIMATE CHOICE

It is not feelings that do damage, but behaviour. You have a choice between behaving constructively and behaving destructively. Destructive behaviour can become a habitual response to stress. Next time you feel under pressure, watch how you behave, and then take control by behaving differently. Being polite to people, giving them an opportunity to sort out problems, exercising tolerance and so forth breaks the vicious circle because it means that others will behave more constructively towards you.

We also have a choice in how we react to larger problems. In the popular thriller *Bravo Two Zero*, author Andy McNab recounts how he was tortured by hostile forces. Starvation and beatings were only the opening salvos. McNab realized that what his captors most wanted was his dignity. This was something they could not take from him. Only he could hand it to them, and McNab resolved not to – come what may.

Contrast McNab's reaction with that of the 'beer can' entrepreneur. Failure didn't do this to the 'beer can' entrepreneur; he is doing it to himself. You do not need to be SAS material to resist successfully. The first step in the 'beer can' entrepreneur's regeneration is to reassert control simply by rising from the settee, removing the empty beer cans and tidying the living room.

There is always a choice, but only you can decide how you will respond.

THE GOLDEN GATE

'Act without expectation,' counsels the Tao Te Ching; 'produce, but do not possess.' These proverbs reflect a paradox. What stresses entrepreneurs is expecting results, expecting success and happiness, their emotional attachment to the business, and the belief that only if they are successful will they command love and respect from others. If you can cultivate indifference to success or failure, not only does stress dissolve but you may actually become more successful because your judgement is no longer clouded by emotion – hence the words of the Zen master, 'not till you abandon all thoughts of seeking something will you be on the right road to the gate'.

Summary

1. Stress results from demands that exceed our coping ability and threaten something important.

2. Stress is debilitating; it is associated with serious illness and early death.

3. Stress also results in poor decision making.

4. The most common causes of stress are:
   - overload or underload, quantitative or qualitative;
   - relationships and responsibility for others;
   - being driven to succeed;
   - major transitions and daily hassles.

5. Stress is frequently accompanied by anxiety and depression.

6. Anxiety produces over-sensitivity to threat, hence 'threat rigidity'.

7. Depression results in perceived helplessness.

8. Depression can be nature's way of forcing you to slow down.

9. Since stress results from lack of control, the antidote is taking charge by:
   - practising time management;
   - installing management systems;
   - prioritizing work;
   - delegating;
   - taking responsibility for yourself;
   - managing expectations;
   - practising emotional detachment.

6

From Good to Great

– crucial decisions

Only a fool holds out for top dollar.

(Joseph Kennedy)

 Key message: The best time to change direction is before you want to

You meet someone attractive at a party. When is the best time to leave?

- 11.30 pm;
- 11.55 pm;
- 12.05 pm;
- when the other person leaves.

Handling success poses a similar dilemma.

It is important because fortunes have been built upon timely changes of direction. It was not luck that made firms like Rothschild fabulously wealthy, but good decision making. More specifically, merchant banks were merchants before they became bankers. In the 17th century, international trade was an extremely risky business. A merchant expecting a delivery of cargo had no way of knowing whether a ship had set sail, far less when it would arrive at its destination. The party exporting the cargo was also exposed to risk as they might not get paid once the ship docked. Entrepreneurially minded merchants discovered that they could earn more money from using their good name to guarantee the bills of lesser merchants in return for a premium than from trading goods and spices. So, they gradually gave up being merchants to concentrate on banking. The rest, as they say, is history.

Jack Scaife earned a good living from selling his dry-cure bacon from a stall in Keighley market in West Yorkshire. Mr Scaife went from good to great by experimenting with an internet business. Turnover soared. Now Jack Scaife's bacon sells in Sainsbury's supermarket. Yet it would never have happened if Mr Scaife had clung to his market stall – successful though it was. The stall is still there and it still sells Jack Scaife's bacon, but Mr Scaife has long since moved on.

THE IDENTITY TRAP

If it is so easy, why doesn't everyone do it? Why don't more hairdressers found chains like Vidal Sassoon? Why don't more doctors open private clinics? Why do vets' opticians' and dentists' practices still operate mainly as cottage industries?

Recall from Chapter 4 that we should select whatever course of action promises the best return for the future, which may mean dropping a successful course of action like being a merchant or running a successful market stall. Recall too that changing direction may entail forgoing past investments – again not always easy.

Yet all else being equal, dropping a successful course of action when a better return on investment becomes available is the correct decision. Moreover, it can mean the difference between being the owner of a small business and founding a phenomenally successful business empire – and often for less work!

Yet it still leaves a question: if it is so blindingly obvious, why don't more owners achieve their full potential? Psychologists believe that the answer to this question may be linked not just to sunk costs but also to identity. Image refers to how others see you. Identity refers to how you see yourself.

More specifically, research by psychologists suggests that identity can prevent us from making crucially important decisions. Firefighters have been known to disobey orders to drop their tools in order to flee a blaze that is out of control. Weighed down by their now useless tools, they end up getting killed. They disobey orders because their tools are the symbol of their identity. Without their tools they are no longer firefighters, so they no longer know who they are. Likewise, trapeze artists have been known to plunge to their deaths clutching their poles rather than save themselves by grasping the wire. They cling to their poles because without them they are no longer trapeze artists, and if they are no longer trapeze artists, then who are they? By the same token, what stops some would-be entrepreneurs from moving from good to great is that the transition means losing their identity. For some people, that is too big a price to pay.

Drop your tools!

DEFINING MOMENT

Making the transition from good to great is not about doing things right or working ever harder, but about doing the right thing; that is, dropping the 'tools'. Electricians will always earn a good living, but so long as they are holding a screwdriver and wearing overalls, they will never become rich even though they are self-employed, because their earnings are limited by the number of hours in the day.

The quantum shift starts with employing people. The object of employing people is simple: to extract a surplus from their labour. A similar principle applies to renting facilities. For example, rather than take the risk of having underemployed staff, some hairdressers rent chairs. Likewise, some dentists rent out surgeries and equipment to associates in return for a percentage of their earnings.

Employing one or two assistants may not be too difficult. The decisive moment arrives when the business reaches a level of maturity such that it requires full-time attention. For some entrepreneurs that's easy, because they want nothing more than to escape from practising their trade or profession.

Others find the transition impossible. What really hurts is giving up the symbols of one's identity. So, like the doomed trapeze artist, the hairdresser clings to the comb, the mechanic to the spanner, the secretary to the computer. Dentists typically make more money from their hygiene assistants carrying out cosmetic treatments than they do from actual dentistry, but relatively few are willing to go a step further and found a chain of practices, because that means letting go of the probe and the mirror.

If identity is holding you back, remember that you do not have to surrender the symbols of your identity for ever. You merely have to lay them aside for long enough to create and maintain something new. There is nothing to stop the celebrity chef who founds a chain of restaurants from working part time in the kitchens. Nor is there any law forbidding the carpenter like David Linley who founds a distinctive brand from periodically wielding the hammer and the chisel. Interestingly, though, once would-be entrepreneurs make the break, few return.

STRATEGY

You will have set up systems to ensure the smooth running of the business and to minimize stress. You will have defined targets to control runaway projects. These moves are what we call micro-management. They are important but not everything. You also need a strategy, a vision of 'what comes next'.

Although it is easy to deride long-term planning as a largely futile exercise because of the black swans beyond the horizon, used cautiously a long-term vision and strategy for the business can act as a kind of guiding star that helps you to stay focused.

Stop!
Think!
Where do you want to be in 10 years' time?

The alternative is to drift from day to day, picking up bits here and bits there, being opportunistic and therefore, ironically, at risk of missing the really big opportunities.

More importantly, while opportunities are themselves black swans, it may not be necessary to wait for them to swim along. Entrepreneurs can be proactive in creating them. Perhaps the most fascinating aspect of strategy is the short to medium term. Decisions about what to do over the next two to three years are as important as the longer-term vision, not least because the timescale is sufficiently short for it to be possible to make a reasonably accurate prediction about what will be. The long term is too far out into the future to be any more than a vision. The short to medium time span is where you can make the biggest difference.

That can mean developing the business and then selling it. Some influential commentators believe that entrepreneurs tend to sell out too soon and for too little. Perhaps, but then there is seldom a perfect time to do anything. Sell shares now and they will immediately rise in value. Yet as Joseph Kennedy, father of assassinated president John F Kennedy and a founder of the family fortune, observed, 'Only a fool holds out for top dollar.' In the 19th century the most successful speculators were those who made their pile and then quit before fortune's wheel turned against them.

When turnover is rising, it is easy to believe that things will get better and better. Almost inevitably, therefore, the temptation is to emulate the fabled Cinderella, who stayed too long at the party.

Quit by half-past eleven.

What differentiates the good from the great is that the latter never try to wring the last drop of value out of an enterprise. They leave that for someone else.[1]

Pat bought a derelict factory for £450,000. He converted it to a health club and sold it for £9 million. Pat's accountant thought the sale was premature. 'You could get a lot more out of this,' he said.

'That'll do me,' replied Pat.

Pat was wiser than his accountant. Rather than try to wring every last drop out of the business, Pat's strategy was to sell while there was still some room for development so that it would be an attractive proposition. Pat's next move, incidentally, was to buy a derelict site for £3 million, the plan being to construct a hotel and sell it on for £30 million after two years.

Use planning to create opportunities.

Notice that there are three elements of Pat's success. The first is a willingness to think about 'what can be'. Where everyone else sees derelict buildings, Pat glimpses money-making possibilities by adding value. He sees what everyone else has seen but thinks what no one else has thought. Second, Pat has a clear idea about what he wants to achieve and the timescale in which he hopes to achieve it. While this does not make him immune from black swans and risk, it provides a focus for his efforts and a clear yardstick with which to measure success or failure. Third, when the ambition is achieved, he quits despite the temptation to carry on.

Pat is successful because he recognizes that the best time to sell a successful business is, metaphorically speaking, like leaving a party; that is, about half an hour before you want to. It requires self-discipline, but self-discipline brings reward.

Summary

1. There is never a perfect time to do anything.

2. Entrepreneurs get rich by employing people.

3. Don't let identity hold you back.

4. Have a long-term vision for where you want to be and concrete short- and medium-term plans.

5. Use the latter to create opportunities.

6. Never try to wring the last drop of value out of a business.

7. The best time to quit is always before you want to.

NOTES

1. I am indebted to Stewart Rayner for this insight and for the example that follows. As always, names and context have been changed to protect identities.

7

Leading the Dream Team

– group decisions

Take counsel.
(St Benedict)

Key message: We may not like
people who challenge us, but we
need them

Success brings new problems. Not least of these is that as the business grows, you will need to rely increasingly upon other people. Understandably, many entrepreneurs find that difficult. You may have built the business from scratch. You have your ideas, your own way of doing things, your own high standards. It is a mistake, however, to continue doing everything yourself. As a 'rule of thumb', when annual turnover reaches £3 million a professional management team is required.

Try to control everything and you will end up controlling nothing.

Management teams can play a highly productive role in decision making because they bring a range of mindsets to the task. Diversity becomes increasingly important as the firm grows, as decisions become more complex and more nuanced. The team must be properly led, however, otherwise it can become a liability. Good leadership requires an understanding of group and organization dynamics.

CULTURES OF CONFORMITY

Diversity is a recipe for conflict. Conflict can be unpleasant and even destabilizing. Indeed, Winston Churchill used to say that all he wanted after quiet and reasonable discussion was his own way! The trouble is, although we may view conflict as an obstacle, it is also a *transaction*, an exchange of perspectives. While group discussion never results in a perfect picture, it is almost bound to be more accurate than what would be achieved by an individual acting alone or in consultation with only one or two other people.

Although conflict is the lifeblood of good decision making, groups have a habit of suppressing it. One way in which this can happen is that the group develops a culture where agreement rather than disagreement becomes the norm. Conflict is productive only if it involves a genuine exchange of perspectives. In mature groups, conflict can degenerate into mere ritual as members occupy predictable positions and articulate predictable arguments. If that happens, group members may think that issues have been thoroughly aired and that the right questions have been asked when they have simply been going through the motions.

For example, Barings Bank continued to operate as if it were a partnership long after the business incorporated. Weekly meetings of the bank's management committee followed a standard format whereby directors each gave a brief report on events in their sphere. Reports were received with polished courtesy. Group norms forbade interrogation or even discussion. If there was to be any argument, then it took place elsewhere. So when, on 6 February 1995, the Barings management committee learned that Leeson's 'risk-free' profits for the previous week were $9 million, a member of the team commented that it was impossible to make such a large amount of money without taking some kind of risk. This was the opportunity to expose Leeson's deception while there was still time to save the bank. Instead, the comment was ignored by other members of the group because conflict was culturally forbidden. After-wards, Barings' deputy chairman, Andrew Tuckey, said:

> It was not our practice with senior colleagues to interrogate them as to what steps they had actually taken to bring themselves into a state of confidence and satisfaction... Our culture was particularly inconsistent with that.
> (*Secretary of State v Tuckey*)

STATUS

Diversity also produces status differentials within the group, which can increase the pressure towards conformity. There are two types of status differentials, ascribed and achieved. Ascribed status refers to the formal status accorded to one's position on the organizational hierarchy. Achieved status refers to one's informal standing within the group as an individual. In theory, all group members may be equal. In practice, some become more equal than others. In some firms, accountants command the highest status, as they control the purse strings. In innovatory or 'high-tech' firms, R&D staff may dominate group discussions. Sales and marketing may be accorded the highest status if they are seen as occupying the boundary between the firm and its customers. Except in a crisis, IT and HR specialists rarely achieve high status.

Such inequalities matter, because higher-status individuals tend to dominate group discussions. In contrast, lower-status members are accorded less 'airtime', and when they do get the chance to speak, other members of the group take less notice of what they say, typically paying more attention to high-status members regardless of the quality of their contribution to the discussion.

It is the quality of advice that matters, not who is giving it.

'GROUPTHINK' AND THE ICARUS PARADOX

In Greek mythology the fabled Icarus flew so close to the sun that his wax wings, which enabled him to fly in the first place, melted, sending him plunging to his death. In other words, what makes us successful can also be our downfall if taken too far.

Without a measure of harmony the group would be dysfunctional. Yet harmony can be taken too far as group members may stop challenging one another for fear of upsetting the cosy atmosphere. Or, as leader, you may tire of the endless arguments within the group and form a small, informal 'in-group' or 'kitchen cabinet' of like-minded and trusted advisers to take the most important decisions.

Be careful! Either way, the group is liable to develop a false confidence in itself known as 'groupthink'. More specifically, 'groupthink' develops when members of the group stop challenging one another for fear of upsetting the cosy atmosphere within the group. When that happens, intellectual rigour is lost and decision making becomes dangerously sloppy. Issues are poorly analysed, there is no attempt to generate a comprehensive set of alternatives, plans are ill-considered, and there is no proper risk assessment and no proper contingency planning. Since no one is issuing any challenge, however, a false sense of unanimity develops. Group members unconsciously say to themselves, 'This must be a good idea if no one disagrees with it.' There is no reality testing, as meetings descend into cosy chats. The result is a false confidence in risky decisions.

Most of what we know about 'groupthink' derives from the public sector. This is not because private-sector firms are immune from 'groupthink'; it is simply that their mistakes seldom become public property. The most famous example of a policy decision ruined by 'groupthink' concerns the disastrous Bay of Pigs invasion of Cuba in 1961 when the US military landed troops on an exposed beach without air cover. The invasion plan assumed that in the supposedly unlikely event of the troops coming under heavy fire, they could retire to caves. An overly confident President Kennedy and his advisers failed to probe the military on the precise location of the caves, which turned out to be separated from the beach by 80 kilometres of jungle swamp. Secure in the comfort of his 'kitchen cabinet', Prime Minister Neville Chamberlain seriously underestimated the threat posed by Hitler. Speculatively, the collapse of Northern Rock bank may owe something to 'groupthink' as the management team must (or should) have known that the bank was consistently running risks significantly above industry standard. Why were they apparently comfortable operating at such a dangerous level?

'Groupthink' can also produce decisions that are ethically questionable. Ethical standards get lowered as the group projects its hostility on to other groups. For example, firms placing contracts with low-cost producers in China and India may pour scorn on competitors who use firms employing child labour earning 20p a day. A group believes itself to be inherently moral and ethically pure because it pays 50 per cent more; that is, 30p a day. It takes an investigation by a Sunday newspaper to shatter that self-serving belief.

Friends are often more dangerous than enemies.

'Groupthink' is also associated with the emergence of so-called mind guards. 'Mind guards' take it upon themselves to shield the leader from potentially disquieting information. Robert Kennedy allegedly became John Kennedy's 'mind guard' as plans for the Bay of Pig's invasion were being finalized. When some members of Kennedy's advisory group began to develop reservations about the invasion plan, Robert Kennedy allegedly told them that the president had made his mind up and that their task was now to support him and not plant doubt.

RISKY SHIFTS AND CAUTIOUS SHIFTS

Experiments by psychologists have shown that groups may take riskier decisions than individuals working alone. The reverse is also possible, known as 'cautious shift'. Groups are also potentially prone to taking up extreme positions (known as polarization) as a result of group discussion, and are thought to be even more prone to escalation of commitment than individuals (see Chapter 10).

It is unclear why groups are attracted to extremes. An influential theory points to diffusion of responsibility. That is, since responsibility for decisions is shared, blame for failure cannot be assigned to an individual and therefore members feel less inhibited about taking risks than they otherwise might.

THE PARADOX OF INTERNAL POLITICS

Politics is about who gets what in the firm, where, when and how. For example, sales and marketing want bigger budgets and bemoan the moneys spent upon R&D, which they argue should be outsourced.

Manufacturing are aggrieved because they perceive themselves to be the poor relations of sales and marketing, who get paid large bonuses. The HR department want a bigger budget for staff training; the IT department argue that money would be better spent on upgrading software. Half of the management team are in favour of closing plant A; the other half think you should leave plant A alone and close plant B.

Often there is no easy way to resolve such conflicts. In theory, resources should be allocated in a manner consistent with optimal decision making. Yet if everyone agreed what the best course of action was all the time, there would be no politics.

Is the answer simply that politics should be banned? Certainly, internal politics can produce bizarre decisions, yet banning politics may do more harm than good in the long run. In the early 1980s two management consultants named Tom Peters and Harold Waterman toured the United States in an effort to discover what made certain firms successful. The results, published in a book entitled *In Search of Excellence*, suggested that the best firms were characterized by a noted absence of politics and politicking.

The story has a sequel, however. Although notions of 'excellence' captured the imagination of a generation of business and management pundits, Peters' and Waterman's firms did not retain the accolade of 'excellent' for very long. The distinguished social scientist Jeffrey Pfeffer has since suggested that it may be precisely because those firms discouraged politics that their lead proved unsustainable.

It is not hard to see why. Although technically a decision fails when expectations are not met, in practice what matters is whether people support it. For instance, a new IT system may match requirements exactly, but if staff do not use it, then it is a failure. Conversely, the system may be primitive, but if staff like it, then it is a success.

As the firm grows, securing support for decisions becomes more important. You may feel that since it is your company, you can do what you like with it. True; but if there is little support for an idea, it should give you pause. If you try to force the issue, people will acquiesce, but the implementation of the idea could well prove to be half-hearted.

Ask yourself, what is the art of the possible here?

It may even be wise to sacrifice some economic efficiency in order to bring potential dissidents round to the wider strategic goal. For instance, when the London Stock Exchange decided to modernize by introducing electronic trading in preparation for 'Big Bang' (deregulation) in 1986, many members protested about losing the traditional trading floor. Rather than defy opposition, the Stock Exchange invested £6 million (1986 figures) to build a new trading floor. It lasted barely six weeks and was eventually closed as even the most diehard traditionalists discovered that it was much easier to sit by a screen than traipse to the Stock Exchange to transact business. Although on one level the concession was a complete waste of money, it proved politic because it made the transition to electronic trading much easier. The beauty of spending the additional money was that it proved beyond doubt the fallacy of traditionalists' arguments – without a shot being fired in anger.

LEADING THE DREAM TEAM: CULTIVATING CHARISMA

Strong leadership can overcome, or at least reduce, the dysfunctional aspects of group decision making and internal politics. Emphatically, by 'strong' I do not mean domineering. For all the millions of pounds and years of effort invested in research, social scientists are still hazy about what makes a good leader. Personality certainly does not appear to be the answer. Management style may make a difference, but it depends on the circumstances.

Recent research does suggest, however, that charismatic (transformational) leadership makes a difference. Transformational leaders encourage followers to extend themselves by accepting new challenges and generally becoming more ambitious. Transformational leaders also score high on consideration for the individual and on their willingness to provide intellectual stimulation.

Followers of transformational leaders are more likely to exert extra effort, and more likely to embrace the values and purposes of the firm and remain with the firm than followers of more mechanistic transactional leaders with their systems of rewards and punishments. Worst still is the laissez-faire approach to leadership, as research has shown that the absence of leadership impacts negatively on followers' willingness to exert extra effort and so forth. I mention it because one can become a laissez-faire leader unintentionally. For example, as the firm grows, you may delegate more and more decision-making powers, perhaps serve on external committees, and, as a result, end up being perceived as an absentee landlord.

Some entrepreneurs may be born charismatic leaders, but charisma can be cultivated. Turn group norms to advantage by positively encouraging lively debate. Do not try to impose a code of conduct but instead get the group to draw up its own. That way, group members are more likely to feel committed to it. Set the tone for discussion by reading it out before the meeting.

An example of a group code of conduct

1. We will listen to one another actively.
2. We will treat each other with respect.
3. We will work as a team.
4. We will be open and honest, without offending, and say when we disagree with something.
5. We will encourage others to speak their minds.

Where possible, avoid extreme status differentials. Failing that, be proactive in stimulating discussion. Solicit the views of lower-status members (and other quiet members of the group) within the group itself but also privately, as they are more likely to speak honestly when alone. Another possibility is adopting the practice used by the military of asking the most junior members of the group to speak first. The assumption is that juniors will speak without being influenced by the views of seniors. The technique is far from foolproof, however, as juniors usually sense what seniors want them to say and respond accordingly.

Vary something.

Throw the group a challenge. Avoid becoming predictable by keeping others guessing — and guessing wrong at that. Where will you sit? What view will you take? Will you be satisfied with progress or will you demand more? Do not hesitate to be firm with the group if the occasion calls for it. If need be, bang the table.

Keep a few tricks up your sleeve such as introducing new members and bringing in outside experts. If the group is dealing with a particularly important decision, keep people on their toes by dividing the group and ask both halves to propose a solution, or assign different elements of a problem to sub-groups. The underlying aim of these tactics is to maintain cohesion while simultaneously challenging the group by altering the dynamics.

Treat important decisions as tentative and revisit them once passions have cooled. Better still, revert to first principles. What was the problem and can it be usefully redefined? The group may have started to look for a solution too soon instead of exploring alternative ways of framing the problem. For instance, if the group originally perceived the metaphorical bottle as half empty, reframe the problem and see what emerges when the bottle is defined as half full. Revisit your information and consider alternative possibilities.

Ask a question – you are a fool for a minute.
Keep silent – you are a fool for ever.

Never be afraid to ask questions. If Barings' management team had probed the precise nature of Leeson's $9 million worth of 'risk-free' profits, the bank might have been saved. If President Kennedy and his team had consulted an atlas, history might have taken a different course.

When the time is right to make a decision, be decisive. Indecision counts as the absence of leadership. It produces confusion and wasted energy. For example, if deciding between A and B, say 'I prefer B'; if refereeing between A and B, say to A, 'I will give you one week to convince B...'

Communicate.

There is no point in making a decision unless people know about it. Develop a system for communicating important decisions and listening to feedback. Moreover, when you communicate, do not just explain what the decision is. Show that you have listened by reflecting back the key arguments for and against; explain why you have chosen option A as distinct from option B and thank people for their contributions.

WALKING AROUND

As the firm grows and your information becomes more refined, do a *little* of what you used to do when you were small: manning the tills, talking to customers, checking stocks and other forms of 'management by walking around'. See it as escaping *to* reality for a while. If Ken Lay of Enron had done this, he might have realized how his managers were ruining the firm that he created. Lay became overly focused on high-level statistics and paper profits and lost touch with 'grass-roots' staff and operations that might have contradicted what his senior managers were telling him. Only a little, mind! Otherwise, you may be sucked back into micro-management. A little, often, is probably best.

Summary

1. As the firm grows, change your approach to match.

2. To maintain overall control, don't try to control everything.

3. Value constructive conflict and try to stimulate it.

4. Seek advice; you don't have to take it.

5. Communicate: ensure others understand the rationale for decisions.

6. It is better to take people with you than have them work against you.

7. Actively solicit contributions from group members.

8. Be unfathomable; keep others guessing.

9. Challenge the 'dream team' constantly.

10. Escape *to* reality occasionally.

8

Get Lucky

– taking risky decisions

Better to be lucky than competent.
(Attributed to Napoleon)

 Key message: Risk is a choice

Popular books about entrepreneurship frequently imply that entrepreneurs get lucky by taking huge risks. This is a MYTH! Most successful entrepreneurs are actually very cautious. They take risks, certainly, but they get lucky by de-risking their ventures as much as possible.

This chapter explains how to approach risky decisions. We begin by reminding ourselves what risk is (and is not) and what attracts us to the wrong kind of risk. We then consider strategies for handling risky opportunities.

WHAT IS RISK?

Intuitively we tend to see risk as the possibility or the probability of something bad happening to us like being burgled, the factory catching fire or suddenly going bankrupt. In this view, things go wrong and there is not much that we can do about it. Yet the word 'risk' actually derives from the early Italian word *risicare*, which means 'to dare'. This definition implies four things:

1. Risk is not a fate but a choice.
2. We choose whether or not to take a risk.
3. We bring most of our misfortunes on ourselves.
4. Risk is something that can, to an extent, be managed and controlled.

WHY BAD RISKS ATTRACT

Being lucky means doing better than an objective analysis of the situation would suggest. A bad risk is a risk that is much bigger than an objective analysis of the situation would reasonably justify.

Imagine an unhappy day at the races. You have lost £95 in failed bets and have just £5 left. Do you bet your last £5 on the favourite running at odds of say 3 to 1 or on a long shot running at odds of 20 to 1?

Logically it makes sense to bet on the favourite as there is a small possibility of emerging with £15 – either that or not bet at all. You may well prefer, however, to risk it all on the long shot even though you will probably only end up with nothing. The decidedly riskier choice attracts because your attention is riveted on the £95 you have lost, and the long-shot bet offers an opportunity to recoup that loss. Recall, however, that the £95 is irrelevant because it cannot influence future outcomes (see Chapter 4). Remove that reference point from the equation and you will see the decision for what it is; that is, a choice of how best to invest £5.

We tend to become risk-seeking when we see ourselves as faced with a choice between losses. To be more precise, prospect theory predicts that faced with a choice between 1) accepting a sure loss at time 1, and 2) the possibility of avoiding that loss altogether but at the risk of subsequently incurring a much bigger loss at time 2, we may be tempted to avoid a sure loss even though we may be risking catastrophe.

Although prospect theory was developed for clear-cut choices involving precise mathematical probabilities, it may well be relevant to many business decisions where the issues are rather more amorphous. Risk-seeking behaviour may explain, for example, why accountants Arthur Andersen ended up being dragged down with Enron, the collapsed energy firm. All that probably happened initially was that Andersen stretched the rules a little. The following year they stretched them a little further, and so on. Taking the ethical path by subsequently refusing the client's demands and/or reporting their misdemeanours would have invited punishment. There is also the possibility that firms like Andersen become caught in the so-called consistency trap. That is, our perceived need as human beings to display consistency demands that having agreed to something in year 1, we will agree to it subsequently. Likewise, a hotelier may be tempted to serve food that has passed its use-by date. More specifically, the temptation is to avoid a relatively small loss by discarding the food. The risk is that the hotelier subsequently incurs a much bigger loss, financial and reputational, if guests suffer food poisoning.

Notice, however, that there is a choice to be made. Disaster is by no means inevitable. The ethical path stands open. There is no law that requires us to be consistent. Nor is there any ambiguity about whether the hotelier should use the food. If disaster happens, it happens through choice. Remember: you make your decisions and your decisions make you.

ON THE REBOUND

We are most likely to become risk-seeking when things are going badly. In the early 1990s, sales of Coca-Cola were declining. 'You can extrapolate that out and end up with zilch,' said Robert Goizueta, Coke's president and chief operating officer.[1] Coca-Cola decided that drastic circumstances called for drastic action and so they tried to reverse their fortunes by changing the formula. The resultant public outcry forced the company to reverse the decision after only three months.

Steiff, makers of luxury teddy bears, made a similar mistake when they decided to compete on price instead of quality and accordingly switched production to China. Steiff thought they had done their homework properly. Indeed, they were prepared for the obvious risks such as safety and poor-quality stitching. It was the more subtle snags that defeated the plan. Steiff did not realize that it would take eight months to a year to train new seamstresses (more used to making microchips) to an adequate standard. Transport costs also proved higher than expected. Ships were frequently overbooked or Steiff would pay premium prices to book space in advance only to find that the bears were not ready to ship. After five years, Steiff abandoned the strategy and moved production back to Europe.

Disappointment can also trigger rash behaviour. Just as the jilted lover frequently seeks a new (and often unsuitable) partner on the rebound, entrepreneurs may react to disappointment by making a very risky move to compensate.

Don't just do something.
Stand there.

Sarah expanded her hairdressing business from a 'one woman' plus occasional assistant, to a large emporium with five chairs to rent to other hairdressers. Sarah discovered, however, that she was actually worse off as a result, as additional revenues were simply consumed by higher rents and other expenses. Disappointed, she immediately decided to open another salon – renting out more chairs to more stylists. A week before she was due to sign the contract for her second shop Sarah changed her mind. She decided the move was too risky:

> I worked it out if I open several shops and make a little bit of profit from each one it could work out quite good but the big risk is the second shop. When you get to the third shop you've already got two shops full of staff and the chance of them both going under is unlikely but when you do your first of two shops [sic], if the staff walked out from this shop for instance I'd have to find £500 a week rent.

Sarah decided to wait a few months and then look for safer opportunities to expand. Not everyone pulls back in time. It was a wise decision because, as Sarah recognized, it is the second venture rather than the first that can be the big opportunity and the big risk. If it goes wrong it can destroy both businesses but if it goes well it can provide the launch pad platform for exponential expansion. So, it pays to be patient and get it right.

MANAGING BIG RISKS

The British Isles have not been invaded often because of the risks involved. The last successful attempt was in 1066 when Duke William of Normandy set forth without so much as a basic 'Sat Nav' to guide him on his way. This daring enterprise succeeded because the astute duke was very careful to de-risk it. First he persuaded Tostig to land a diversionary force in the north of England ahead of the main invasion. Second, after the Battle of Hastings William kept his ships within hail as he progressed through southern England.

Be bold but cautious.

Like Duke William, many successful entrepreneurs are bold in their ideas but cautious in executing them. Business analysts predicted that Richard Branson's decision to enter the aviation industry was doomed to fail. Branson, however, was careful to de-risk the bold decision by leasing rather than buying planes so that if it went wrong his exposure would be limited. Things might have gone better for Coke if they had done some small-scale market testing of their new brand rather than taken a 'big bang' approach.

De-risking can take many forms. 'Just-in-time' delivery arrangements can reduce the risk of incurring a cash flow crisis by minimizing the cost of holding stock. Buying a franchise can reduce start-up risks. Forming a consortium can spread risk among several parties. Another possibility is to use a counterbalance by combining high- and low-risk elements. For instance, opera houses staging works by obscure composers counterbalance the risk of empty seats by engaging well-known performers likely to attract the crowds.

THE PATEL STRATEGY

Of course, you cannot de-risk everything. Ultimately there is nothing for it but for entrepreneurs to 'play their cards and take their chances'. One of the most famous risks taken in business history was Tom Spencer's decision to invest his life savings in Michael Marks's small retail empire. Marks had already come a long way in a short time from his days as an itinerant pedlar selling buttons, thread and other small items from a small tray when he met Spencer. Moreover, Spencer must have been impressed by Marks's success and his energy and ambition. Even so, it was a big risk. There was no welfare state in those days so Spencer would have been destitute in old age if it had gone wrong. As we now know, the risk paid off handsomely. While Marks worked to death running the business and opening new stores, Spencer retired to the country and rapidly drank himself to death on the proceeds of a business that still bears his name even though he never actually worked in it.

High risk: high reward = good
Low risk: high reward = better.

Although high risks can be justified by high reward, there is another, possibly better, way to get rich known as the Patel approach. The Patels had very little money so they concentrated upon buying cheap motels where the profits were good, the risks of failure low and the financial consequences containable. Eventually the Patels built a chain of motels all over the United States and as a result became extremely wealthy. It is the difference between the 'hare' and the 'tortoise'.

KEEP YOUR OPTIONS OPEN

Why do we fit locks on doors? Unless you are an economist or a police officer you have probably never given the question a moment's thought! Intuitively you might say, 'to stop people from breaking in'. Yet locks are only fitted if the trouble and expense are justified. After the suicide bomb attacks on the London Underground in July 2005, an alert police officer checking a property noticed that a new and expensive padlock had been fitted to an old garden shed. Why go to all that trouble, reasoned the officer; what did the shed contain that was worth protecting? The officer's curiosity was rewarded with the discovery of a stash of explosives.

Like fitting locks on doors, options theory assumes that there is economic value in resolving uncertainty and capturing opportunities. An option creates the right but not the obligation to take an action in the future. For example, if you manufacture orange juice you may want to know what you are going to have to pay for oranges in a year's time. It is a tricky question because so much can change meanwhile. Rather than try to guess the price and risk getting it wrong, you could purchase an option that gives you the right to buy say 10,000 tonnes of oranges in a year's time at 10p each. If in a year's time oranges cost 9p, the option expires, worthless. If the price of oranges has risen to 11p, however, the option is exercised and the party granting it stands the loss. Whatever happens, you can be sure that you will pay no more than 10p for your oranges.

Options are most commonly used where business revolves around currency exchanges or involves dealing in commodities, but they can be deployed in a variety of contexts. For example, Hewlett Packard chose a portfolio approach in designing printers. That is, rather than guess which type of input slot was likely to prove most popular and risk getting it wrong, HP decided to incorporate all four industry standards into the design. The purchase price of the option in this case is in higher production costs. The pay-off is increased consumer appeal. Likewise, an entrepreneur might purchase an option to buy out a partner, or to abandon R&D ventures, or, like Branson and his planes, use leases to defer full investment.

Options are also a way of exploiting opportunities. There is seldom opportunity without some kind of risk, but, by definition, opportunity is the flip side of risk. For instance, many initial risky investments, such as opening up operations abroad, create follow-on possibilities for further expansion. Expansion is not compulsory, but should local conditions favour it, the entrepreneur can increase manufacturing capacity or diversify the range of products made. Whereas a firm that concentrates its operations in a single location must cope with all the turbulence and uncertainty that arises there, a firm that is spread geographically can transfer activities from one location to another.

There are five different types of options:

1. immediate entry;
2. immediate exit;
3. delayed entry;
4. delayed exit;
5. shadow option.

Let us consider each in turn.

IMMEDIATE ENTRY

An immediate entry option involves advancing a small amount in order to create or acquire the right to purchase a full commitment later. For example, placing a deposit on a car buys you the right but not the obligation to purchase the vehicle in the future. You simply lose your deposit if you decide not to proceed (though an entrepreneur would probably sell his or her place in the queue at a handsome profit!).

Immediate entry options are particularly valuable where a decision is time-critical or dependent upon exclusive rights. Apple clinched a two-year lead over competitors by securing the rights to miniature hard drives central to the iPod music player design. Employing people on work experience programmes is another form of immediate entry option. Such programmes enable you to test prospective employees before deciding whether to employ them. (Incidentally, another benefit is that potential employees are more likely to return to a firm if they have worked there before.) A firm with a fledgling factory abroad might acquire options to buy land should they subsequently wish to expand.

IMMEDIATE EXIT

An immediate exit option involves making a full commitment but acquires the right to reverse it immediately. For example, rather than take the risk of employing engineers, a software development company may hire them on a consultancy basis. While this is a more expensive solution than employing people, if a contract is cancelled or work dries up for some other reason, the company can immediately rid itself of surplus staff. Likewise, some landlords rent office space and industrial units on an immediate exit basis. The rents are higher than traditional leases but the corollary is that the tenant may only be required to give a week's notice.

DELAYED ENTRY

Delayed entry options are useful where entering and exiting the market involves an expensive 'all or nothing' commitment. Oil exploration companies, for example, may decide to acquire the land and the necessary licences but postpone drilling until they have conducted detailed geological investigations. The advantage of paying for such an option is that subsequent decisions about whether or not to drill are based upon much better information than would otherwise be possible. Likewise, a speculative builder might acquire land banks cheaply in the midst of a recession but delay construction unless and until property prices reached a certain level.

DELAYED EXIT

Whereas a delayed entry option allows you to buy time before making an expensive investment, a delayed exit option allows you to buy time before abandoning a project. Delayed exit options are useful where exiting from a venture is so expensive that the decision is virtually irreversible. For example, if the price of say gold or diamonds falls to such a level that mining no longer makes economic sense, rather than close down the mine completely and sell off the land it might be wise to mothball it pending developments. It costs money to keep the mine in commission but it is much cheaper than opening a completely new one. Delayed exit options proved popular during the so-called credit crunch of 2009 as many construction companies decided to mothball plans to build flats and houses.

SHADOW OPTIONS

Shadow options emerge unexpectedly. A vet assisting in a branch surgery learns about how to run a business as well as gaining clinical knowledge and experience. Suddenly the principal decides to sell. The assistant's experience makes the option of buying the business much less risky than it would otherwise have been.

Shadow options can work the other way, too. Sam owned an antiques business for many years. As fashions changed, the business gradually became non-viable and Sam eventually sold the building he owned. He was then invited to manage an antiques business for someone he had known as a competitor for many years. 'It's great,' said Sam. 'I shut the door and go home. I don't have to worry about anything.'

Sam's career as an owner created this shadow option. Firms that share knowledge and experience informally can create a 'shadow option' by paving the way for joint ventures. Such firms may have a flying start compared to firms that plunge into the unknown.

We are all what might have been.

Even failure can create a shadow option. For instance, shelved R&D projects can re-emerge. Attempts in the early 1980s to create small handheld computers capable of reading handwritten text were complete failures. Yet these prototypes eventually became the commercially successful Palm Pilots of the new millennium.

Although shadow options emerge unexpectedly, entrepreneurs can get lucky by purchasing a few. Bunker Hunt (mentioned in the Introduction) did precisely that when he bought the drilling rights to a marginal oilfield that no one else wanted. Recall, Hunt saw the purchase of an option as an additional 'card' to play. Entrepreneurs can increase the number of 'cards' in their hands by investing here and there, diversifying a little, becoming involved in some committees and so forth. After all, what are time and money for, if not for risking? Many if not most potential shadow options will fizzle away. The point is that almost certainly one or two will come into the money.

CAVEAT EMPTOR

Options encourage entrepreneurs to address fundamental sources of uncertainty rather than merely hoping everything will turn out for the best. That said, options cannot solve all problems of risk and uncertainty. Moreover, they come at a price and, since they are difficult to value, they may not always be worth what you paid for them. Consultants may insist upon a guarantee of a fixed number of days' work a year, thus obviating part of the value of an immediate exit option. The risk, moreover, may not always be confined to the initial purchase price of the option. For instance, in practice, switching production from one country to another can be a complex and problematic exercise. Keeping an option open like a mine or an oil platform may require ongoing investment. Delayed exit options may provide an excuse for escalation. Pursuing shadow options can deflect energy and resources into sideshows that detract from the pursuing of a coherent strategy. Indeed, purchasing lots of small options may be more costly than living with the uncertainty. Ultimately it is a case of *caveat emptor* (let the buyer beware).

Even so, used carefully, options are a potential weapon in the entrepreneur's armoury against risk. The best way to manage options is to be specific. Investigate carrying costs, be clear about what needs to happen before an option is exercised, and ensure that the capability exists to support the option meanwhile. For example, specify in advance at what price a partner will be bought out. The alternative is to be left haggling later.

The value of options increases with uncertainty. Shadow options are perhaps the most interesting of all because they can occur by chance as well as design. Indeed, you could perhaps say that all of life experience is a potential 'shadow option' that might one day be exercised.

Summary

1. Risk is a choice.

2. To be risk-seeking is to take a bigger risk than circumstances warrant.

3. Risk-seeking behaviour may be triggered by loss or disappointment.

4. Entrepreneurs take risks, but they de-risk ventures as much as possible.

5. Be bold in conceiving ventures but cautious in executing them

6. High risk may be justified by high reward.

7. Low risk and high reward is even better.

8. It may be worth using options to limit risk and capture opportunities.

9. Shadow options may be worth more than you think.

NOTES

1. Whyte, G (1991) Decision failures: why they occur and how to prevent them, *Academy of Management Executive*, 5, pp 23–32 citing Camaniti (1987)

9

Be What You Can Be

– decisionless decisions and the psychology of success

No one could suspect that times were coming... when the man who did not gamble would lose all the time, even more surely than he who gambled.

(Charles Péguy)

Key message: Taking too little risk can be worse than taking too much

It is afternoon at the market. Fruit vendors are calling, 'Pick your own bananas! Twenty pence a pound! Come on now, ladies! Pick your own bananas!' Another stall-holder shouts, 'Margarine! Plenty of margarine!' It starts raining. A trader grapples with plastic sheeting to protect his stock. His neighbour advises him not to bother. 'You can't damage damaged goods!' he jokes.

Beneath the banter lurks anxiety. Before, being a market trader was a sure route to prosperity, particularly for a trader in the indoor market. Times have changed, however. January and February were known as 'kipper months' because of the quiet post-Christmas trading. Now almost every month is a 'kipper'. Gone are the days when flower-sellers carried their takings home in buckets and spent all of Sunday counting out the copper and silver coins and when grocers could pile their counters high with pork pies and expect to be sold out by 5 o'clock. 'Stalls [in the indoor market] were like gold dust,' said a trader. 'You couldn't get one for love nor money.'

Now, hardly a week passes without another trader pulling down the shutters for good. 'This stall is in a good position,' said a trader, 'but what can you do when people aren't even stopping to look?'

What indeed? Significantly, it is often the most prosperous traders who have suffered worst. We will explore later why that is the case. Here it is sufficient to note that whereas the previous chapter concerned excessive risk taking, this chapter considers:

- why too little risk can be even more dangerous than too much;
- what makes us afraid of risk;
- how to overcome fear of risk.

THE PSYCHOLOGY OF SUCCESS

Which would you prefer:

- a sure gain of £500,000; or
- a 50 per cent chance to win £1 million or, alternatively, nothing at all?

Most of us would probably opt for a sure gain of £500,000 because although it is a lot less than £1 million, it would enable us to do important things like paying off a mortgage, providing for school fees or providing a comfortable cushion in retirement.

Supposing, however, the choice were between:

- a sure gain of £10,000; or
- a 50 per cent chance to win £1 million?

Unless we are absolutely desperate for £10,000, the optimal choice is to gamble on winning £1 million. Although it is risky, because you could end up with nothing, the risk is justified by the potential reward.

Yet it is a risk that not everyone would take. Prospect theory predicts that gains that are certain tend to be preferable to those that are merely probable even though the latter may be much more valuable than the former.

If you are consistently successful, is it because you are not taking enough risk?

Prospect theory may explain why some entrepreneurs stop short of achieving their full potential and why some highly prosperous businesses eventually melt down. In a nutshell, the theory implies that entrepreneurs may hesitate to take risks for fear of jeopardizing what they already have. Indeed, this is what stops many people from becoming entrepreneurs in the first place: fear of giving up a nice, steady job.

Peter owned four stalls in an indoor market. He made a very good living. The chance arose to acquire a stall in a market 20 miles away. This was in the days when stalls were like gold dust, and Peter decided to proceed. The experiment lasted barely a fortnight. 'This is doing my head in,' said Peter's assistant.

'It's doing my head in too,' replied Peter, so they walked away.

In retrospect, Peter believes that the decision to quit was a mistake. 'I see now that I could have branched out from there but at the time I was afraid that it would pull me away from my main line of business.'

You can't make an omelette without breaking eggs.

Peter's fear of becoming distracted is tantamount to a fear of endangering existing gains. Such reluctance can affect big, sophisticated firms too. For example, Goldman Sachs enjoyed a huge run of prosperity during the 1980s. In the early 1990s, many partners were reluctant to experiment with new ventures such as government bonds. Why upset the golden goose?

Goldman Sachs... was highly successful and the partnership was by its nature conservative. After a decade of astounding prosperity, the impetus for change was low. 'We were moving too slowly or not at all, to face some serious competitive threats... If we waited to fix them it might get too late.'[1]

The firm was only propelled into those new markets thanks to the determination of two far-sighted partners, Stephen Friedman and Robert Rubin, who recognized that current levels of prosperity were unsustainable. 'If you are not constantly working for constructive strategic change, then you are steward of something that must erode,' said Stephen Friedman.[2]

ON A ROLL

The proverb states that a bird in the hand is worth two in the bush. In business, however, as Friedman and Rubin recognized, the *apparently* safer option may not be safe for very long. No law guarantees that an existing line of business will be viable for ever, however prosperous it may be and however rock-solid certain that prosperity may seem.

Sam made a fortune from opening up shops on short leases, closing them down again when the lease expired and opening up somewhere else. Sam describes the business in its heyday:

> You'd get there with the staff about quarter past six in the morning and by half past seven people were in the shop and they were buying... I'd say possibly that queue would be 35 people long – all the way round that counter out into the street... till half past four – it was non-stop... you were literally run off your feet... The wholesalers... once or twice they'd open up for us on a Saturday... because you just couldn't get enough... [stock] in the shop... I couldn't have done better if I'd won the [football] pools.

The first ominous note was sounded by Sam's accountant. He asked Sam where he thought the business would be in 10 years' time. Sam said:

> I was flying high at that point. I said, 'What do you mean?'
> He said, 'Where do you think you'll be in 10 years' time?'
> I said, 'Well, I hope I'll still be in business and making a living.' But you do, you think it's never going to end.

But it did end. Within less than 10 years, as supermarkets put many small shops out of business, Sam ended up with only one outlet and only a fraction of his former wealth.

> *Doing nothing is a risky decision.*

Recall, risk is a choice. Sam could see no reason to change his business model as he was making a fortune. Yet doing nothing, 'business as usual', is itself a risky choice. It is what we academics call a 'decisionless decision'. Decisionless decisions have consequences, just like any other decision. Outcomes – for better, for worse; for richer, for poorer – are determined by inaction as well as action.

ENTRAPMENT

The trouble is, the impact of 'decisionless decisions' becomes apparent only when it is too late to reverse them. Continuity begets continuity. Entrepreneurs can become trapped in a sub-optimal venture through the simple passage of time. Entrapment happens because time is an investment and one that is every bit as important as money – possibly more important in the long run.

In the 1950s, Val's hairdressing salon was the epitome of elegance and luxury: white net curtains, white wood furniture offering a temporary escape from the omnipresent dirt and damp of a sooty town and houses with cold taps, stone sinks and outside toilets. It was a thriving business with both sinks and all four driers in regular commission.

Forty years later the business was still going but generating barely enough money to keep Val in a modest standard of living. It was not hard to see why. The upholstery of two chairs was split. One sink looked as if it had not been used for years – a picture of rust, cobwebs and grime. The towels looked tired. The white plastic 'curlers' were covered in a grey, greasy film of dirt. The walls and surfaces were damp and had patches of black mould. The electrics were the original 1950s, yellowing and probably dangerous. The net curtains had been transformed from white to black. The years had taken their toll on the client list too, as death and population movements had reduced the numbers little by little.

> *How does a business decline?*
> *One day at a time.*

The decline was partly due to Val's decision not to employ staff. Recall, employing people is an important route to prosperity because you can extract a surplus from their labour. Val was risk-averse. She did not want the bother of possibly having to get rid of staff, so she took the apparently safer option. Compounding the decline was Val's tendency to hide behind the net curtains, ignoring new hairstyles and treatments, instead carrying on with the familiar perms and 'shampoo and set' that she felt safe with.

As Val's story shows, there is a price to be paid for remaining within one's comfort zone – whether it is technology we understand or business practices that have worked well in the past. Furthermore, once a business begins to decline, the process becomes progressively harder to reverse because a vicious circle is set in motion. As the business declines, funds for reinvestment become scarcer. It therefore becomes harder to retain customers and attract new ones. Consequently, the decline deepens. Eventually the business becomes a shadow of its former self, living on borrowed time.

Some big firms also hide behind metaphorical net curtains. Marks & Spencer clung to their tried and tested formula long after high street retail practices had moved on. It took the imminent threat of meltdown to persuade management to offer customers facilities such as changing rooms and the acceptance of external credit cards. More recently, Woolworths paid the ultimate price for seemingly being trapped in a terminal time warp.

THRIVING ON FEAR

Fear holds us back more than anything else. To calculate the opportunity cost imparted by fear, list all the things you would do if you were not afraid.

What would you do if you were not afraid?

The first step in shrinking fear is to identify what you are afraid of. Be specific: fear feeds on vague terrors.

What exactly are you afraid of?

Having isolated the problem, then deal with it. There are two schools of thought. One is to 'feel the fear and do it anyway'; the other is to wait until you feel reasonably comfortable about making a move and then make it. Both approaches have something to recommend them. The advantage of the former is that by doing, you will probably make the fear vanish. The risk is that if you are really afraid, you may not do it very well and end up failing as a result of fear. The advantage of acting with a fair degree of confidence is that you are more likely to succeed. The disadvantage is endless procrastination. If possible, combine both approaches. Again, the 80/20 rule is a good one. That is, wait until your very worst fears have subsided, feel the residual 20 per cent fear and then do it anyway. You should analyse the market before launching a new product. The danger is that you can analyse the market for ever. So, do some analysis and then try to achieve your first sale.

DIY RISK ASSESSMENT

Another technique for confronting fear is to conduct a risk assessment. Risk assessment works by listing all the main risks that you can think of surrounding a venture and then multiplying probability and impact to arrive at a risk score.

Imagine you are considering acquiring a company. Your worst fear may be that the acquisition becomes a cultural misfit with your existing operations – a risk that is quite high because of the differences between the two operations. So, you score the likelihood of that risk becoming a reality as 7 out of 10. Next, consider the possible impact of the risk. It could be quite significant as most mergers between large firms founder on cultural tensions that destroy rather than create value. So, you score it as 8 out of 10. Now multiply 7 by 8, making a total risk score of 56 out of 100. When you think about mitigations, however, you realize that you could organize the takeover in such as way that everyone, including staff in your own firm, has to apply for their own job. That would create an opportunity to exclude cultural misfits and remove poor performers from your own firm. On the other hand, you have to ask yourself whether the cure would be worse than the disease. That is, would the resultant tension and uncertainty precipitate a meltdown of both firms – a very serious risk if a 'people' business is involved? On the other hand, can you afford to let this opportunity pass you by? If you don't do this now, where might you be in 10 years' time?

Risk assessment checklist

List all the main risks involved in a venture.

1. How probable is this risk on a score of 1 to 10?
2. What would the impact be on a score of 1 to 10?
3. Multiply the two results to achieve a risk score.
4. What could I do to reduce the probability?
5. What could I do to minimize the impact?
6. What might be the cost of not taking the risk?

Risk assessment is a useful weapon in decision making but it is by no means foolproof. Risk has a sense of humour. You may think you have covered all the major risks and then the unexpected happens. Moreover, risk assessment is an inherently subjective exercise because there is little objective guidance on how to assign numbers to probabilities and impacts. Even so, working through the process does at least reduce risk and quantify vague terrors.

SPECULATING TO ACCUMULATE

Being wrong about something can be a Very Good Thing. If you play the National Lottery, you are almost certain to get it wrong but that does not mean that the decision to invest a pound is a disaster. Far from it! Where the stakes are small and the pay-off is sufficiently large, we should carry on investing even though we accumulate failure after failure.

Fear of being wrong often prevents us from seeing opportunity – the flip side of risk. Fear of being wrong is deeply ingrained in us from school onwards. The 'ticks and crosses' approach to learning instils fear and ignores shades of grey. When Marks & Spencer opened their store on London's Oxford Street in the 1930s it was by no means certain that the venture would be profitable. The decision went ahead, though, because the company reckoned that even if the store made a loss, having a presence in such a prestigious location would benefit the chain as a whole.

ADAPT AND SURVIVE

Town and city markets may have declined but there is still money to be made. The most promising survivors are typically those who have moved with the times, making small but significant, low-risk changes to the business such as replacing old, greasy, handwritten signs with brightly coloured laminates, investing in a new display, experimenting with new lines, listening to customers, and picking up ideas for adding value from trade magazines and trying them out.

The attraction of this strategy is that it avoids the much bigger risk involved in completely revamping the business. Some ideas work, others don't. The point is, any losses are small and therefore the damage is limited. Moreover, a series of small changes can add up to more than the sum of their parts.

Always provided that you are willing to 'give it a go', that is. Michael was a successful fishmonger who owned a large house and a Bentley. Michael had been selling fish all his life. The shop was taking over £50,000 a week. He recalls how his daughter started badgering him to start selling new lines like bass and sea bream in addition to the traditional cod, haddock, plaice and kippers. Michael refused to hear of it. He then went on holiday, leaving his daughter to run the business:

> I remember going on holiday and I left her in charge. All the time she's been saying we ought to get all these [new] fish. 'Oh! No! No! No! — too dear.'
>
> I came back and I remember the bill was about 25 per cent more than it had been [in] the previous weeks before we'd gone on holiday. I looked at it and she'd bought all these things. I didn't know what she'd taken at that point, but I thought, 'Oh crikey! It's going to be a disaster is this.'

Notice what happens here. The business is taking £50,000 a week and Michael is worried about a few extra boxes of fish. The point is, even if the experiment failed, the risk was justified given the level of turnover. Michael, however, is more afraid of risking existing gains than excited by future possibilities. Besides, the experiment succeeded. Michael again:

> And it hadn't been [a disaster]. Then you realized, people wanted other things; they wanted bass and they wanted squids and they wanted prawns. I would say now that probably without [new lines] we wouldn't be able to survive at the rents and rates that we pay and the cost of staff.

Moral: do it.

The market traders we most wanted to interview were the ones who were no longer there; that is, those who sold up when stalls were still like gold dust. How did they recognize that the metaphorical clock was turning half-past eleven? Did they, like Pat in Chapter 6, have a plan to quit or did they read signals that others ignored?

We will probably never know the answer. One possibility is that they looked at return on capital employed as well as the more usual yardsticks of profit and turnover. If you have say £100,000 invested in an enterprise and the annual profit is £5,000 (5 per cent), you would actually be better putting the money in the bank if it would earn 6.5 per cent there. Lowering of return on capital employed can be an early warning sign that midnight is approaching.

THE DANGERS OF HERDING

A word of caution: don't do something just because everyone else is doing it. Why do Harry Potter books sell millions? The reason may well be because millions have already been sold. Economists call it herding. Imagine a row of restaurants. They are all empty except one, which contains two diners. You might decide that the latter probably has something to commend it as two people have chosen to eat there. So you follow suit, and so do the next couple and the next. In each case the decision to eat there is made on an assumption rather than hard information about the quality of the food.

Resist the temptation to follow the herd. Members of a herd are not making informed decisions and could therefore be heading over a cliff – like the banks caught up in the sub-prime mortgage market. As the market for conventional mortgages became saturated, banks looked for alternatives. They started lending to people whose credit ratings would not otherwise qualify them for a loan. Other banks followed suit – ignoring the precept that the art of banking is to lend money to customers who can afford to repay the loan, not to charge higher rates of interest to people likely to default after two or three years. Beware also computer herding. One of the reasons why banks all end up ensnared in the same mess is that they all use the same software programs to analyse risks and make investment decisions.

Fortunes have been made by moving in the opposite direction to the herd – selling when others are buying, investing when others are holding off and so on. During the run-up to deregulation (the Big Bang) in 1986, most of London's traditional broking and jobbing firms scrambled to find buyers among the giant US investment banks – with Cazenove as a notable exception. The firm's partners stood largely aloof from it all, reasoning that there would be a market for truly independent advice in the post-Big Bang era. The influential *Financial Times* newspaper disagreed with this assessment and predicted that Cazenove's independence would prove short-lived. In fact, Cazenove survived and prospered for 15 years before finally merging with J P Morgan.

QUANTUM SHIFTS

Adaptation has limits. The stagecoach companies and canal boat owners of old responded to the threat posed by competition from railways by instituting express services that raised their 'game' from around 6 kilometres an hour to around 16. The strategy was successful for a while because rail travel was initially slow and unreliable, but ultimately the earlier forms of transport were doomed.

Stick to the knitting, but not for ever.

Nothing is immune from time's erosion. We will always need teachers, but many university education departments in the United Kingdom became virtually redundant when the government changed the method of training. We will always need dentists, but improved standards of living and better health education mean that we need far fewer. There will always be criminals, but lawyers who specialized in criminal law, expecting a comfortable living, have found their livelihoods undermined by reductions in legal aid payments.

Profound change cannot be halted, but the effects can usually be anticipated by engaging in simple scenario planning. What would you do if X, Y or Z happened?

It pays to think the unthinkable occasionally.

GO HIGHER

The unthinkable does happen. Sam's business was prosperous but its prosperity was built upon sand. The most enduring entrepreneurs create a legacy. This means more than owning a string of businesses and dabbling in all manner of investments from slot machines to recycling paper clips.

Be what you can be, promises the US army recruiting slogan. Why not create something unique like Anita Roddick's Body Shop, Tim Farmer's Kwik Fit or James Dyson's vacuum cleaners? It may be no more work and no more risky or difficult than mere ownership. It will not render you immune from competition, copying of ideas and time's erosion, but there is the pivotal advantage of being first in the field, to say nothing of the satisfaction of inscribing your signature.

Summary

1. Taking too little risk can be as bad as taking too much.

2. Risk aversion arises from fear of endangering existing gains.

3. We are most likely to be risk-averse when we are already successful.

4. Ask yourself what you would do if you were not afraid.

5. Consider feeling the fear and doing it anyway.

6. Small adaptations can add up to more than the sum of their parts.

7. Think long-term. Remember, nothing is for ever.

8. Beware herding.

9. Go higher: found a legacy.

NOTES

1. Endlich, L (1999) *Goldman Sachs: The Culture of Success*, Time Warner, London, p 88. The speaker whose words are quoted is Stephen Friedman.
2. Endlich, *Goldman Sachs*, p 188

10

Decisions about 'Runaway' Projects

– The escalation trap

If at first you don't succeed, try, try again. Then quit.
No use being a damn fool about it.

(W C Fields)

 Key message: Persistence is a virtue.
Don't let it become a liability

- 'That's the hardest part, accepting that it's never going to work.' (An entrepreneur)
- 'I kept saying, 'Can't get any worse. No, it just can't get any worse.' But it does. It gradually gets worse and worse' (An entrepreneur)
- 'You don't go into business to give in.' (An entrepreneur)

No one should expect to get it right all the time. Recall, if you are consistently successful, you could be missing good opportunities because you are not taking enough risk. Risk, of course, implies the possibility of failure. If a venture appears to be failing, you may have a very important decision to make. Do you reinvest or quit?

It is said that there are no hopeless situations, only people ready to declare situations hopeless. If entrepreneurs were not willing to persist despite poor odds, we would have far fewer businesses. The trouble is, if a venture is ultimately doomed, persistence will only make things worse.

Bunker Hunt's foreman (see the Introduction) could not resist drilling down another 3 metres. He was lucky, as he struck oil. Yet supposing the attempt had proved abortive. The foreman might well have ended up drilling down another 3 metres, and another 3 metres, and so on – a phenomenon known as escalation of commitment.

To be more precise, escalation refers to persistence with a failing venture beyond an economically defensible point. Research by psychologists suggests that rather than halt a failing venture, entrepreneurs are likely continue investing time, money and effort long after it has become obvious that there is little prospect of success. Escalation is dangerous because it results in wasted time and effort, blocks learning and can turn a mistake into a calamity. This chapter explains what causes escalation and what entrepreneurs can do to protect themselves against becoming caught up in an escalatory spiral.

THE DILEMMA

In theory a venture may be deemed to have failed when feedback from the market reliably indicates that expectations are unlikely to be met. In practice, feedback is seldom so obligingly loud and clear. To a point, therefore, escalation is just a normal business expense – but only to a point!

Jan and Pam, who were sisters, bought a café. The café was a present from Pam's husband paid for out of a lottery win. The seller owned several businesses. He claimed that the café was becoming too much for him to manage. The accounts showed that it was taking £1,500 a week, making an annual turnover of around £75,000. 'I'm not bothered if it doesn't make a profit,' said Jan. 'It's just summat to do. You get a laugh, especially when the lorry drivers come in.'

The two sisters took over in June and set to work. They cleaned and redecorated the premises, reduced prices and dispensed with the services of a surly assistant whom they suspected was stealing from the business — 'ripping off the tills blind,' said Pam. The sisters also instituted new dishes like curry and risotto. They even installed an attractive chill cabinet to display cold drinks. 'We've given the place a clean, decorated, brought prices down, tried to be friendly, tried new things – now it's up to them [customers],' said Jan.

The chill cabinet lasted barely three months. 'That didn't do any good so it had to go back,' said Jan.

The creative cooking initiative did not do any good either as customers kept coming back to pork dinners and pork sandwiches. The sisters were also dismayed to discover that the café attracted 'all day sitters'; that is, people who buy a cup of tea or coffee and literally try to make it last all day. They are usually people from local care homes, sometimes drunk, sometimes with poor personal hygiene, and they drive away other customers, including the relatively lucrative lunchtime trade. In addition, Jan's husband was frequently writing cheques from his lottery winnings to balance the books.

They paid £28,000 for the business. 'It were never worth it,' said Pam.

'What do you think it's worth?', I asked.

'Maybe twenty-two thousand,' said Pam.

'I reckon we'd be lucky to get eighteen for it,' said Jan.

Has this business well and truly failed? It has certainly proved to be a disappointment, but can we safely say after only three months that there is no prospect of expectations being met? After all, the business only has to break even. Perhaps trade is poor over the summer months and will improve as Christmas approaches.

THE PSYCHOLOGY OF ESCALATION

Faced with such equivocal feedback, what can entrepreneurs do? Research suggests that escalation is frequently driven by a desire to protect our ego. In more colloquial language, we are likely to persist with questionable ventures like the café rather than admit failure. We may therefore be slow to accept that a venture is never going to work, and carry on investing because we simply cannot believe that we have made a mistake.

As feedback worsens, we are likely to lapse into denial. Denial can take many forms. One is to downplay the threat. For example, when cheap imports of cloth began arriving in the United Kingdom in the 1950s, the mill owners declared that there was no cause for alarm. As the trickle became a flood, mill owners continued to insist that there was no cause for alarm. Another form of denial is to persuade ourselves that the problem is temporary, or that things cannot get any worse. Alternatively, we may blame the problem on factors that are beyond our control such as the weather, currency fluctuations or the price of oil. A common thread running frequently through all of these self-serving beliefs is that trade will soon recover or that success is just around the corner, given just a bit more money and a bit more time.

Self-deception resides in how decision makers process their information. Feedback from the market usually contains a mixture of positive and negative data. We tend to notice and pay more attention to the positive while downplaying or even ignoring the negative. For example, if sales are up one week or if there is an upsurge in enquiries about our products, we may jump to the conclusion that our problems are over when these indicators may well prove spurious – mere straws in the wind.

Since such biased processing occurs unconsciously, we may genuinely believe that things are not nearly as bad as an objective analysis of feedback from the market would suggest. The most extreme form of denial is known as 'bunker mentality'. When his dream of a thousand-year Reich crumbled in the face of advancing armies, Hitler literally retreated to his bunker deep beneath the streets of Berlin and rapidly lost touch with reality – issuing orders to an army and an air force that had long since been obliterated. 'Bunker mentality' among entrepreneurs can manifest itself as shying away from newspapers and trade magazines reporting unpalatable information – like the growth of cheap foreign imports; postponing meetings with the accountant; refusing to open envelopes containing bank statements, bills or other bad news – until a sharp shock forces them to recognize reality. By the time the bailiffs arrive, however, the damage is well and truly done.

AUDIENCE EFFECTS

Even if we privately acknowledge that a venture is hopeless, we may feel driven to persist rather than admit failure publicly. The desire to maintain appearances before family, friends, accountants, competitors and so forth can be powerfully conducive to escalation:

> It may be even more difficult for entrepreneurs than others to face the
> ridicule and loss of face that can stem from admitting they were wrong in

the first place; this would be especially true with respect to bitter recriminations from friends, family and early backers – people who bought into the entrepreneur's dreams and now find that these have crumbled.[1]

To demonstrate the power of social pressure to my MBA students I offer a pound coin for auction. There is no reserve price, so in theory it is possible to obtain the coin for as little as one penny – with one condition, that is. A special rule of this auction is that the second highest bidder must pay the bid price and they receive nothing. The auction is great fun as students enjoy making mischief, ramping up bids. Inevitably two bidders end up trapped in an escalatory spiral where the only way out is to admit defeat. Consequently, the coin is always sold for significantly more than its face value.

Business ownership offers many opportunities to become ensnared in the same destructive dynamic, whether it is airlines and supermarkets fighting price wars or 'barrow boys' vying with one another to achieve the biggest turnover. For example, one Christmas George astonished competitors by buying 25 1-hundredweight (51-kilogram) bags of sprouts on sticks to sell on his market stall. The sprouts occupied a whole corner of the stall and took two men all day to sell. 'And you know how much we made,' said George? 'Twenty-five pounds! We would have been better just buying five bags and selling for a fiver each.'

'LOCK-IN'

When we finally do recognize the need to quit, we may discover that our problems are only just beginning! We may be confronted by a warehouse full of stock, redundancy costs, penalty payments, the cost of removing partially completed works, and obligations under a lease.

After a year, Jan and Pam decided to quit the café. 'You've got to give a new business time,' said Jan. 'We've tried all sorts, but if you're not getting anywhere after a year...'

Accordingly, the café was put up for sale. Weeks passed and there were no takers. Then a bombshell dropped. The landlord pointed out that under the terms of the lease, they must pay £30,000 to transfer ownership.

Economic ties can make quitting almost as expensive as continuing. Peter discovered this when he considered closing his shoe factory in Portugal. Initially, the factory had prospered at the expense of UK firms, only to be undermined by competition from China and Taiwan.

For Peter, closure meant disposing of estate, plant and machinery, cancelling contracts, disposing of work in progress, to say nothing of making the workforce redundant. Peter decided it was too much trouble. He kept the factory open even though he knew that persistence was sub-optimal.

The risks of escalation are heightened when decision makers are liable to be held personally responsible for failure. This observation becomes increasingly important as the business grows and professional mangers are appointed to help run it. Managers required to account for potentially expensive mistakes may decide that they have nothing to lose by pouring more and more of the firm's resources into failing ventures.

WHAT ARE YOU GETTING INTO? PREVENTING ESCALATION

Once an ill-advised investment is made, it becomes progressively harder to change direction. Preventing escalation is therefore better than cure. Before committing yourself to a decision, think about what you may be getting into. It may seem trite to say 'read the contract before you sign it' – but Jan and Pam did not afford themselves this luxury. Likewise, before instructing lawyers, think about escalating costs – on both sides. Do you really want to risk becoming entangled in a protracted dispute – bearing in mind Voltaire's comment that he was only ever ruined twice? Once was when he lost a lawsuit. The other time was when he won.

Try to envisage how a decision might play out in practice. I have heard many rueful tales told by entrepreneurs about taking on contracts that turn out to be barely profitable, only to find they are contractually and/or morally bound to seeing the job through to the bitter end. Be especially careful where the work is complex and/or laborious and the projected profit margins are thin to begin with.

He who rides a tiger can never dismount.
(Chinese proverb)

Resist the temptation to react when competitors throw down the gauntlet. In particular, avoid being drawn into price wars and other mutually destructive competitions, like boasting about turnover. Stay focused upon your own targets and ambitions. By all means reduce prices if market forces so require, but do it for the right reasons.

DEFINE EXPECTATIONS

A decision fails when results are consistently below expectations. Entrepreneurs who are careless about defining expectations deprive themselves of a potential early warning system. The solution is simple: define expectations, precisely and in detail, in advance. Time is money, so set timescales for the attainment of expectations too.

Demand results.

Entrepreneurs may be slow to recognize sub-optimal ventures because they have no clear idea what level of profit and turnover they expect to achieve over a given timescale. Entrepreneurs who specify results are likely to make more money than their more passive colleagues. Tell yourself that if you are going to work hard and take risks, it is going to be for something!

COMMUNICATE

As the firm grows, it is important that managers and employees understand your expectations. While they will absorb a certain amount by osmosis, there is no substitute for promulgating the message. For instance, if projects are time-critical, everyone needs to know that deadlines are to be taken seriously. The alternative is a complacency culture where projects slip little by little and the only person worried about it is you!

MONITOR PROGRESS

Install a system that enables you to track progress against expectations. Many entrepreneurs who go bankrupt do so because they lose sight of basic information. Don't dump the responsibility on to an accountant. Be proactive and make sure that you should know where you stand financially and on other important parameters from month to month, week to week or even day by day.

You don't go bankrupt if you know you are going bankrupt.

A crisis means that all the self-serving myths that exist in your head are no longer tenable. Face facts; if expectations are not being achieved, take action before creditors descend. That way, you at least exert a measure of control over the situation.

SET LIMITS

Set limits on how much time, money and effort you are prepared to reinvest in a faltering venture. The precise nature of those limits is a personal choice that will depend upon a range of factors such as the state of the economy and the industry; possible alternative investment opportunities (see Chapter 4), financial constraints and your personal circumstances. For instance, you may decide that under no circumstances will you put your house at risk.

Identify quitting points. Again, it is a personal decision, but you might decide, for example, to wait six months or a year to see whether turnover improves. Here is how Carole made a crucially important decision:

> Year on year we were getting less profit. Originally we were able to [save but] not this Christmas gone... We had enough to pay everything off – but we could not put anything away. So it was really at that point we could see the writing on the wall – that we had to make some kind of decision about this because things were not going to get any better and eventually we would have been faced with dipping into our savings to pay our expenses. So that was what pushed us.

Carole avoids the temptation to retreat into denial. She faces up to the knowledge that the business is declining. She sets limits; her savings are sacrosanct. When her savings are threatened, she quits.

No good setting limits and quitting points unless you abide by them. Almost inevitably, the temptation is to wait just a little bit longer or, metaphorically speaking, to drill down another 3 metres. You have to draw a line somewhere. There is almost always a chance that things will get better. It is a case not of being right or wrong but of choosing the lesser of two evils. Carole again:

> We didn't want to get to that pitch that we were desperate and we had nowhere to turn. We felt that if we made the choice now then we do actually have some choices. We haven't put every last penny into the business; we've still got savings and if we want to invest those savings in another business then we can do that.

It was a hard decision but it was the correct one because it meant that Carole lived to fight another day. Remember: you make your decisions and your decisions make you.

BUDGETS

Budgets can be used as a tool for setting limits. For example, in the pharmaceuticals industry, developing new drugs is so risky that projects are only funded one phase at a time. The project is then reviewed at the end of each phase of research and development. A further budget is allocated only *if* feedback from clinical trials and other relevant data justifies further investment. In other words, projects have to prove their worth or they are automatically terminated. It is an interesting way of preventing escalation because it removes fear of failure, as the expectation is that only a minority of projects will make it to market.

A word of caution: research by psychologists has shown that using budgets to control expenditure can produce the opposite error to escalation. More specifically, research has shown that decision makers can be reluctant to reinvest if told that the budget has been expended. By itself, budget depletion should never be a reason for cancelling a project, because it constitutes what accountants call a non-informative loss. That is, budget depletion merely indicates that a certain sum of money has been expended. It says nothing about the state of the project and future pay-offs. The risk, however, is that good projects are terminated.

This observation also applies to the informal allocations we make in our heads. Just as we budget so much for gas, so much for electricity and so forth, we construct mental budgets for the time and effort we expect to expend on our various projects. Again it is a mistake to abandon a venture just because it is taking longer or proving harder than originally estimated. These too are non-informative losses and should be treated as such.

CHANGE THE APPROACH

If a decision fails, try again. If it fails again, don't give up but ask yourself why it keeps failing. What are you doing wrong?

If you keep doing the same things, you will get the same results.

Essential learning cannot happen if you refuse to acknowledge that there is a problem or if you blame failure on factors like the weather or currency problems or the machinations of unscrupulous others. For instance, is the business in the wrong location? Is the marketing weak? Are economic trends running against you?

Then stop repeating the mistake.

DON'T TAKE IT PERSONALLY

Try not to take failure personally. The venture may have failed; you haven't. All business ventures are basically experiments. They may not use test-tubes and Bunsen burners, but they are voyages into the unknown nonetheless. Scientific experiments frequently fail but that does not make the scientists who design and conduct them failures. Scientists treat failure as a normal part of the exploration process. They learn from it and move on.

All business is an experiment.

The parallel holds good for business. Every one of Richard Branson's bids to operate the National Lottery failed. Moreover, failure happened in the full glare of publicity. Yet no one sees Branson as a failure. Branson set limits. He decided that if the third bid failed, he would abandon his pursuit. Likewise, when his bid to take over the collapsed Northern Rock bank was rejected, he simply turned his attention to the possibilities of entering the private health care market instead.

An entrepreneur whose business failed said, 'I don't feel like a failure in any way. I just felt disappointed because to me it's the best thing I've ever done... Even though it didn't last long.'

A month later this entrepreneur reopened in a better location. For all I know, I may have been speaking to a nascent founder of an international business chain like Marks & Spencer or McDonald's.

MINDS ARE FOR CHANGING

Christine had practised successfully as a sole practitioner solicitor for many years. She then agreed to take two colleagues into partnership. The prospects were good, as Christine explains:

[H]e [the prospective partner] was very competent and had got quite a good following. He had in his practice a young solicitor... a very personable young man who was also fed up with his firm. We thought he could take some of the low-level work off me. We decided that we should keep both offices going for the time being and gradually build up the practice. It seemed like an ideal situation.

On day one, Christine tried to telephone her partners at 3 pm. There was no reply. She subsequently learned that they had taken the staff from their office to a champagne lunch. Christine was angry:

It was my practice. These people were out at my expense... time that they should have been in the office... You would have thought that on day one they would have been very keen on... getting things sorted out.

Christine began sending her bookkeeper on invented errands to her partners' office. It soon became clear that long lunches were the norm. Christine said:

As days went by, my bookkeeper... never seemed to find any of them there. People used to phone up and say, 'I can't get any reply from your office in _____.' This is at 3.30 in the afternoon.

It was the same excuse every day. The partners claimed to have got back five minutes later or to have been delayed seeing a client. Christine was worried:

> I thought the Law Society could get involved and say there was some-thing seriously amiss with the office... I would lose my reputation that I had worked hard to build up... I would lose my client base. It did cross my mind that they could have been taking money out [stealing from the practice].

The firm had been in existence for just six weeks when Christine received a telephone call from the senior partner of a large City firm who had been unsuccessfully trying to contact Christine's partners. The caller threatened that unless he received a reply within half an hour, he would report the matter to the Law Society. Christine said, 'I thought, if I don't do something quickly, I am going to lose everything.'

When the partners returned from lunch, Christine summoned them to her office. She told them what had happened and then said, 'It's not working out, is it?' From that moment the partnership was dissolved.

There is no law that requires us to be consistent. If an ill-judged deci-sion threatens something important, reverse it immediately. Although Christine felt somewhat foolish dissolving the partnership having just advertised it and having had new cards and headed notepaper printed, her livelihood was at stake and so she was right to take drastic action. Forget social and cultural pressure that tells us to keep right on to the end of the road and finish what we have started. You can change your mind; that's what minds are for.

Other people may be surprised, shocked even by your volte-face, but it is like the sinking of the pride of the British fleet, HMS Hood, in 1941. One moment it is unthinkable. The next it has happened. Besides, no decision ever goes completely according to plan. Military command-ers may have a plan to 'take that hill' but they are forever adjusting it to take account of emerging circumstances. There is no disgrace in doing that. In fact, the lives of troops may depend upon it. Why should busi-ness be any different? Indeed, to be inconsistent is to be unfathomable, and to be unfathomable is a competitive weapon in business as well as war.

Incidentally, Christine's doubts proved to be well founded as she subsequently discovered misplaced documents, clients' money in the wrong place, cases neglected, documents not filed in time and partners failing to keep an appointment in court for which Christine subsequently incurred liability. Christine said:

I think they thought they were out for an easy ride. They knew I had a good practice. I think they thought they would just... pick up the cheque at the end of the month without putting any substantial effort in.

Christine's intuition that her partners might have been stealing from the practice was also uncannily accurate. A few months later the personable young man was struck off for stealing £20,000 from an elderly client.

DECIDING WHAT TO REWARD

At the risk of sounding cynical, if a venture goes awry, you must expect managers to be economical with the truth. Step into their shoes; what would you say? Listen to their reports carefully. What do phrases like 'reasonably comfortable' mean? What is missing from the account, what are you *not* hearing?

On a more positive note, consider whether you should reward your managers on process rather than results in order to prevent 'runaway' projects. Rewarding for process involves assessing managers on how they approach decisions. For instance, have they identified the obvious risks, and what mitigations have they put in place? Are feedback mechanisms fit for purpose and is subsequent action timely and appropriate?

The argument for focusing upon process is that it removes fear of failure and therefore the motivation to conceal failure by escalating. The danger is that it can lead to a so-called tick box mentality whereby managers go through the motions, receiving information, holding meetings and so forth comfortable in the knowledge that their salaries and bonuses are assured provided that they make it look as if they are doing the job properly. The result, moreover, may be to reward people who consistently fail to deliver anything. Rewarding results provides a clear motivating force, and after all it is results that count in the end. The downside is the danger not only of escalation but of sliding into unethical and even illegal practices, as evidenced, for example, by the collapse of Enron.

Consider taking the middle way by reviewing both results and process. What has been achieved and how was it achieved?

NOT INVENTED HERE

Finally, let me return to the risks of erring in the opposite direction to escalation. Budgets are not the only problem. Research is scant, but conceivably the psychological and social pressures thought to drive escalation may well be reversible.

Ego-defensiveness can blind us to good ideas. For instance, entrepreneurs may reject someone else's invention out of hand because since they did not think of it, they assume it cannot be any good! In a merger or takeover you may be negatively biased against incumbent staff because you did not appoint them. So, you underestimate their capability and end up wasting talent that you have paid good money to acquire.

Be careful too about publicly threatening to pull the plug on faltering projects. While limit setting is generally a good thing, economically viable projects should not be terminated just because you feel honour-bound to carry out your threat. Yet in experiments, people have done precisely that!

Moral: a good decision maker has no ego.

Summary

1. Instead of exiting failing ventures, entrepreneurs may be tempted to escalate their commitment.

2. Escalation can turn a mistake into a calamity.

3. Escalation is thought to be mainly driven by fear of failure.

4. Sometimes it can be almost as expensive to quit as it is to continue.

5. Prevention is better than cure: be careful what you get into.

6. Set precise expectations and timescales for their attainment before committing resources.

7. Monitor progress regularly.

8. Used properly, budgets can help prevent 'runaway' projects.

9. Set limits on your involvement, identify quitting points and stick to them.

10. Don't take failure personally. If an idea doesn't work, try something else.

11. No law requires you to be consistent. Be unfathomable.

12. Beware erring in the opposite direction to escalation.

NOTES

1. Baron, R A (1998) Cognitive mechanisms in entrepreneurship: why and when entrepreneurs think differently than other persons, *Journal of Business Venturing*, 13, pp 275–94 at p 288

11

Negotiated Decisions

My word is my bond.

Key message: Don't get mad,
don't get even, get what you want

Negotiation is about getting what you need to run the business at a price
that makes economic sense. It is a form of interactive decision making
aimed at improving your situation where the balance of power between
the two parties may be highly asymmetric. Clearly, seldom will you be
able to walk into a supermarket and negotiate a reduction in the price of
tinned beans. Nor are you likely to find it rewarding to haggle over the
price of coffee in Starbucks. Yet many if not most commercial transactions *are* negotiable, even those marked 'non-negotiable'.

This chapter explains what to do when, for example:

■   the price is too high;

- the offer is too low;
- someone makes unreasonable demands;
- something you need is 'not for sale' – at any price;
- the response is 'take it or leave it';
- the other party calls the whole thing off.

THE KEY TO SUCCESS

The key to successfully negotiated decisions is to be clear about what you are trying to achieve by negotiating. This means distinguishing between interests and positions. A position is an inflexible demand such as:

- 'I won't take a penny less than £350,000 for the business.'
- 'We want a 10 per cent wage rise.'
- 'The doors *must* be 15 centimetres thick.'

It is possible to negotiate over positions. Indeed, many decision makers do precisely that. The outcome is likely to be better, however, if you negotiate over interests instead. Imagine dividing a bag of cherries between two people. Ostensibly, the simplest and fairest approach is for each party to take half. Supposing, however, you explore the interests of both parties – why do they want the cherries? It emerges that A needs the fruit to bake a pie. B wants the seeds to fill microwavable equivalents of hot-water bottles. There is no reason, therefore, why A cannot have all the fruit and B all the stones. Negotiating over interests produces an outcome that doubles what would have been yielded by negotiating over positions.

Interests are not always obvious, however. They have to be explored, probed and discussed. Indeed, part of your task as a negotiator may be to make the other party aware of their interests.

Price is not everything.

Price is important but it is seldom the only interest at stake. For instance, a prospective landlord may be aiming for £1,500 a month rent for the premises. Yet would he or she rather have a tenant who pays £1,500 for three months and then defaults, leaving the place in a mess, or a tenant who pays £1,450 a month regularly and keeps the premises in good order? Or let's suppose that you have a consignment of old machinery to sell. While extra cash would be useful, it might be more important to clear the workshop sooner rather than later even if it means giving the stuff away – if there are larger interests at stake.

There may be conflicting interests in negotiations but there are usually shared and/or mutually compatible interests as well. Suppose you are buying second-hand office furniture. Price matters because you need to make a small sum of money go a long way. Yet so does quality, as the furniture will be on view to customers. Your time is also valuable. Ideally you would like to purchase everything you need from one supplier rather than trail all over town seeking out a cheap chair here and a cheap desk there. Now consider the seller's interests. Large orders are usually preferable to small ones. Miscellaneous furniture is harder to sell than matching suites and sellers are nearly always keen to sell old stock.

Now think about how those interests might coincide. You want to save time. The seller wants to move a large quantity of stock – so there is common ground between you. Since your cheque might represent six months' rent, and since the purpose of negotiating is to improve your lot, the seller may well agree a discount if asked.

Yet a discount may not be in either party's best interests. More specifically, supposing you buy £3,000 worth of goods, then it might be reasonable to seek a 10 per cent (£300) discount. However, suppose the seller has some large mirrors for sale at £100 each that could be deployed to enhance your office. You might ask for four mirrors instead of the discount. The seller may well be amenable to this suggestion because although the normal selling price is £100, the mark-up on each mirror is £50 so your suggestion only costs them £200 – cheaper than a discount. Moreover, you get four mirrors where you would otherwise have had only three, so both parties end up better off.

Stop!
Think!

What do I want?
What do they want?
What do we both want?

WAVING THE MAGIC WAND

Inventing options where both sides benefit can make the difference between success and failure. Lateral thinking can help in the task of identifying solutions. Lateral thinking involves stepping back from the problem and re-examining potential blocking assumptions. Imagine a hen trying to reach a bowl of food on the other side of a wire fence. The hen pecks away energetically but fruitlessly. The blocking assumption in this case is that 'the problem' is getting through the wire fence. No: the problem is to reach the food on the other side. Redefining the problem enables the hen to consider other options that were not immediately obvious, like circumnavigating the fence.

Mark could not understand why Ken refused to sell his electronics business. Ken was now in his late seventies; surely he would jump at the chance of securing a comfortable retirement? Yet no matter how much money Mark offered Ken for the business, the answer was always the same: 'no'.

Step to their side.

Eventually, like the hen stepping back from the wire, Mark stepped back from his obsessive pursuit of acquiring the business and explored what lay behind Ken's apparent obduracy. It then emerged that Ken's wife had recently died and that Ken dreaded the prospect of a lonely retirement. Ken also felt guilty about the prospect of parting with the firm because his father had started it in the early 20th century when commercial applications for electricity were in their infancy. An entrepreneurially minded engineer 'desperately interested in electricity', Ken's father bought 60 telegraph poles more or less on impulse and subsequently used them to create a primitive form of cable wireless, charging subscribers a fee of 1s 6d a week (7.5p) to connect up. Selling the business would constitute a final break with a family tradition. Learning of this, Mark suggested another option whereby Ken would retain a share in the business and continue working in it as a consultant. His offer was accepted.

HANDLING PRICE

Although price is only one factor in the equation, it matters. The aim of negotiating is not to drive a hard bargain but to protect yourself from making a bad one. There are two key problems:

1. What is a fair price to pay?
2. How to handle unreasonable demands?

Ignore the seller's price tag. Otherwise, you may be misled by the so-called anchoring effect; that is, basing estimates upon information supplied. For instance, if a consignment of wood is priced at say £4,000, anchoring theory predicts that negotiations will be centre around that figure even if it is a complete nonsense. Likewise, research has shown that surveyors (although they deny it) subconsciously base their estimates of property values on the asking price.

DO YOUR HOMEWORK

Knowledge of market rates is a powerful weapon when negotiating a price. For example, if the market rent for industrial units is £600 a month and a prospective landlord is seeking £695, ask them to justify the figure – 'Where do you get the extra ninety-five pounds from?'

Don't tell them they are wrong.
Ask why they think they are right.

Instead of telling the other party they are wrong, get them to explain why they think they are right. No one likes being told they are wrong; let them discover it for themselves by asking questions. For instance, if a customer demands doors 15 centimetres thick as against an industry standard of 10 centimetres, don't try to argue them into submission; ask them why they need the additional thickness.

Be open to reason but don't yield to pressure. If a supplier claims that you owe them money and threatens to sue, don't just reject their claim ('see you in court') but say something like 'I am not trying to avoid my obligations. I would like to understand why you believe I owe you this money.' Asking questions enables you to exert control over the relationship without committing you to anything. Moreover, it means you can expose the flaws in the other party's argument without antagonizing them.

Alternatively, you may emerge with a better understanding of the other party's point of view. The landlord may acknowledge that the going rate for a unit is £600 but then point to additional facilities or potentially favourable terms within the lease. That does not mean that you pay the additional cost. You might say that while you accept in principle that better facilities should command a higher rent; you are not convinced that those facilities justify an additional £95, and then make them a counter-offer.

Supposing the other party says that they have specified a thickness of 15 centimetres for extra security. You can then reframe the problem: 'So, do I understand you correctly, thickness is a means to an end and your interest is in security?'

Notice what happens here. Asking a question changes the focus of the discussion from a position to an interest. You might then explore what the doors need to be secure against; are they to be arson proof, bomb proof, nuclear attack proof? The next question might be whether there is a cheaper and/or more effective way of achieving that objective.

HANDLING HARD BARGAINERS

Of course, some people will try to knock down a price just for the sake of it. The trick is to not to argue but to move the discussion on to other factors like quality and reliability. The other party are probably expecting an argument. This tactic confounds their expectations and upsets their game plan. You may use better materials than your competitors, and/or you may have invested in better equipment. Make sure the other party understands what their money buys if they deal with you. If that fails, try something like 'Certainly I can do you a cheaper price. I'll come over and see you and we can go through the specification together and you can show me where you want me to cut corners.'

Likewise, if the other party changes their mind and asks for significant changes to the specification that were not priced into the original contract, say something like 'Yes, we can do this additional work but there will be implications.'

This is the genteel approach. With some people it may be necessary to be more direct. 'Yes, of course you can have additional things in the design over and above what we originally agreed. Let me know what you want and I will work out a price.' That will probably be the last you hear of it!

Hard bargainers can also be expected to continue extracting concessions so long as they sense you might be willing to make them. Signal an end to the game by making a very small concession.

Incidentally, from the buyer's standpoint, fixed-price contracts are generally preferable to contracts based on time expended and materials used. 'Time and materials' contracts are by definition open-ended. It means that liability is unknown as there is no control. Indeed, such contracts are so open to abuse that they are often called 'a licence to print money'. Fixed-price contracts are by no means foolproof either as the contractor may be entitled to claim additional payments for unforeseen eventualities. For example, if an employee accidentally cuts through a cable and work grinds to a halt, the contractor may be entitled to claim for lost wages and other expenses, and similarly if work has to be halted because excavations reveal a Roman temple. Moreover, unscrupulous contractors may submit artificially low bids in order to win work. The difference, however, is that whereas with a time and materials contract the bill simply gets bigger, the contractor has to justify additional costs and the client may refuse to pay ('you are experienced, you should have allowed for this').

As contractor, of course, it is in your interests to agree a 'time and materials' contract. Since the other party are unlikely to welcome the suggestion, much will depend upon their perceived alternatives and your reputation and antecedents. Be particularly careful where novel technology is involved. BAE Systems almost floundered over the Astute submarine project that it agreed to build for a fixed price. This highly innovative venture (one of the claims made for the Astute was that it could lie submerged in the English Channel and eavesdrop upon the *Queen Elizabeth II* in New York) went massively over budget when BAE's computer-aided design system proved hopelessly inadequate for such sophisticated command and control systems. Eventually the contract was renegotiated because it was in no one's interests for the project to fail. Even so, the damage to BAE was severe.

For large-scale ventures it may also be wise to negotiate an agreement for interim payments to be made for work successfully completed rather than carrying the whole cost of the project to handover. If doubt exists about a buyer's ability (or willingness) to pay, it may be wise and reasonable to demand payment up front.

GETTING PAST 'TAKE IT OR LEAVE IT'

Recognize that a non-negotiable 'take it or leave it' position is itself a negotiating ploy. So is the buyer or seller who appears uninterested, who is too busy to talk to you or who has another customer. Such stratagems are designed to lower your expectations and hurry you into an agreement that might not be in your best interests. See it as a game; there is always another customer, and with careful handling almost everything is negotiable.

Sometimes it pays to be bold. For instance, if you are buying a car the salesman or woman will probably retreat into trade guides and tap furiously on a calculator when asked to name figures. The purpose of this ritual (and it is a ritual) is to lend an air of scientific objectivity and authority to the derisory sum they are about to offer in part exchange for your vehicle. Change the game. Take the lead by naming the price at which you will deal before they even open their trade guide. They may not like it because you have seized the initiative and nothing in their training handbook has prepared them for it. No matter; the experience will do them good and save you lots of money.

One bold move sometimes carries all before it.

Consider the following case study I use with my MBA students:

> A laptop computer is displayed on an outdoor market stall. The price tag reads '£200 NO OFFERS'. How would you approach the owner to negotiate a lower price?

One tactic is to just to ignore the price tag and make an offer. The risk with this approach is that, having already dug an emotional hole for him- or herself by posting the notice (recall Chapter 10), the seller might react angrily and refuse to deal at any price.

In situations where the other party has become entrenched, the indirect approach often works best. When companies post sales literature, they seldom telephone to ask for an order directly. The opening gambit is usually to check whether you have received the brochure, whether you have had time to study it and 'what did you think of it?' This is the indirect approach; the enquirer is feeling their way, testing the water before posing the vital question.

If the front door is closed, try the side.

Returning to the laptop computer, you might begin by looking at everything on the stall except the laptop. Browsing cables, printers, hard drives and so forth will attract the owner's attention and interest. Eventually the seller will probably ask you what you are looking for:

> 'A laptop, actually...'
>> 'Got one here, mate...'
>> 'Oh yes...'

Continue at an oblique angle by asking questions. Talk about specification, warranty (highly unlikely, given it's a market stall) and so on, but don't mention the price! Look tempted but doubtful. You are not sure whether the machine is powerful enough for your needs. Perhaps you would be better off with a new machine. The owner might offer to sell it for less. If he or she does, the non-negotiable taboo is broken. You then make a counter-offer.

Indecision is a good sign in negotiations. If the other party seems doubtful yet not dismissive, press your advantage. Remind them of their interests. Express confidence that you will reach an agreement. Make success seem close by emphasizing how little separates you from an agreement. Repeat your offer, reach out your hand and invite them to shake it. Better still, tempt them by holding out the money in your hand...

Failing that, you might try to negotiate accessories free of charge. Another possibility is to ask the owner to justify the price: 'Before I give up, I would just like to understand where you get that £200 from.'

If you meet a steel door – retreat.
If you meet mush, drive on.

ASK FOR WHAT YOU WANT

Knowing what you want is only half the battle. The other half is being prepared to ask for what you want. Consider the greengrocer whose consignment of bananas were not the Class 1 product that he paid for. He says:

> I buy bananas from _____, supposedly a reputable firm — supposed to be Class 1, but they were what you call repacked. Once the seal of a banana box has been opened, once the air gets in, it's got to be sold. It had been repacked — open two days, so obviously it wasn't worth the £13 that we'd paid for them. But it's how you go about making it right. So what do you do? Do you go back to the wholesale... and throw these boxes at someone because you're angry, or do you go back and say, 'Mark, three of those four bananas we got on Saturday were repacks?' and hope that he says, 'We'll sort it out.'

It is always a good idea in negotiations to imagine being the other party. How would you react if someone threw a box of bananas at you? They might refund the money but refuse to have any further dealings with you. If that happens, both parties lose. A reputable supplier would very likely offer to 'sort it out'. If not, say, 'Please would you make good.'

In many negotiating situations, buyers and sellers have discretion to vary prices. Bank managers may have discretion to waive charges if the customer has been poorly served. Estate agents may have authority to reduce their commissions from 1.5 per cent to 1 per cent if that is what it takes to win the business. Wavering local authority environmental health officers may be persuaded to award three stars for hygiene instead of two. Even the tax office may allow a few days' grace before levying fines — if asked.

If you don't ask, you don't get.

If the other party has discretion, your task is to get them to exercise it; why pay more than you need to? If necessary, ask for what you want. They can only say 'no'.

Make sure, however, that you are talking to the right person. People on the lower echelons typically have the power to say 'no' but they may not have the power to say 'yes'. Don't deal with them; if need be, go to the very top.

KEEP THE INITIATIVE

Good negotiators rarely say 'no' no matter how ridiculous the proposition seems. Instead, they will either make a counter-offer or say 'maybe' and promise to think about it.

Why say 'no' when you can just as easily say 'maybe'?

In negotiations, as in war, it is an advantage to possess the initiative. The problem with saying 'no' to an idea is that it cuts off communication and returns the initiative to the other party. The advantage of making a counter-proposal is that it moves the discussion on to your terrain. Saying 'maybe' buys time to think of other possibilities, and of ways of expanding the 'pie'. It is also a gentle way of lowering expectations.

GET WHAT YOU WANT

Negotiating can involve riding an emotional roller coaster. People get angry and impatient, take offence and may even call the whole thing off. Don't waste time reacting to criticism, or take offence, or plot revenge. Stay focused upon what you are trying to achieve. Think of anger as an unaffordable luxury. If necessary, break off the discussion for a while to allow emotions to cool.

Think before you act.

Anger blinds us to our interests. For instance, Zita was a subcontractor for a major training company. After four years the company said they would not be renewing her contract. No reason was given. Zita was annoyed. Her first instinct was to terminate her relationship with the company there and then. As she was about to finalize a piece of work, however, Zita realized she would be in breach of contract and therefore might not get paid the substantial sum owing to her. Since that was not in her interests, she decided to stay her anger. She would finish the work and then respond. As her anger cooled, however, Zita realized that actually it was in her interests to maintain an amicable relationship with the company as it might help her win work in the future.

Anger is a spiral.
Let it exhaust itself.

If the other party becomes angry, get them to tell you their story. If, having told it, they are still angry, get them to repeat and continue repeating it until the anger has dissipated. Alternatively, wear the other party down by moving in harmony with them:

■ 'I can see you are angry.'
■ 'I would have been angry too.'
■ 'It is frustrating.'
■ 'I would be sorry if you called the deal off, but you must do what you think is right.'
■ 'I understand your concern.'

Telling the other party to do what they think is right usually gives them pause and stops them from doing something rash. The technique works because the purpose of calling something off is revenge, to restore the other party's esteem. Acknowledging that you will be sorry if the deal collapsed restores their esteem, while telling them to follow their own inclination signals that you are not going to be manipulated.

The words 'I understand' can have a very powerful effect in negotiations. Sometimes people just want to be listened to.

If negotiations promise to be tense, invest time in building rapport before getting down to business. A useful tactic is to begin by asking a few simple questions that the other party will have no difficulty in answering, and then proceed to agree upon a few small things first, like uncontroversial things such as coffee breaks and finishing times.

THE POWER OF PATIENCE

It is axiomatic in negotiations that those in a hurry make poorer deals for themselves than those who take their time. The skilled negotiator sees time as a weapon to be deployed whenever the opportunity arises. For instance, if you plan to buy say a consignment of 1,000, take your time. Begin by asking the other party what they would charge for an order of 800. Let the other party do the work like checking prices and availability; it helps to create a 'sunk cost' effect (see Chapter 4) so they will be all the more reluctant to see you walk away.

It was St Teresa of Ávila who said, 'Patience obtaineth all things.' Patience matters because time can transform the balance of power in a relationship, causing one party to become stronger and the other weaker.

Money flows from the impatient to the patient.

If the other party stands firm, let reality teach them a lesson. Every day a property stands vacant, the landlord loses money. Every day that the laptop computer remains unsold, it becomes more obsolete and exposed to risk of theft and damage in transit. Towards the end of the month, car dealers' minds become increasingly focused upon their bonuses. If they are a few sales short of target, they may be prepared to sell at cost (or less) because it is now in their interests to do so.

Patience is also the key ingredient of persuasion. Persuasion works by giving the other party time and space to consider their interests.

Plant an idea.
Let it grow.
Water occasionally.

Hannah and George bought a castle and converted it into a restaurant. The business thrived and eventually won a host of accolades. Hannah and George had been in business for about 15 years when a large company offered to buy the castle. Since the company were interested only in the castle and not the restaurant, the money offered was far from compelling. Hannah and George tried to negotiate but the company stood firm. The representative left his calling card, however. Over the ensuing weeks, Hannah and George then did some thinking. Yes, the money was a lot less than they would have liked. On the other hand, they were weary of the '24/7' commitment of ownership. They also knew that another local restaurant had been on the market for years and was still unsold. Should they ever need to sell, Hannah and George reasoned, they too might find themselves trapped. Moreover, if they sold, they could have a long holiday (the first in years) and then start another business. After considering their wider interests, Hannah and George decided to accept the offer.

No one can think if they are being continuously bombarded by telephone calls, text messages and e-mails. It is essential to leave the other party alone. Moreover, when you approach them again, do so gently ('Just wondering if you have had any more thoughts about...').

A DASH OF PRAGMATISM

For all that has been said about not giving in to pressure, in some situations a pinch of pragmatism is required. Pragmatism means recognizing reality. More specifically, power in negotiations rests on the cost to both parties of *not* reaching an agreement. This is why there is usually no point in trying to negotiate the price of a tin of beans. If you decide to walk away, the cost to the supermarket is negligible, as they will have no problem in selling the beans to a more amenable customer, whereas you have to spend time tramping round another supermarket.

Where the cost to you of not reaching an agreement is high, it may be in your interests to stretch a point. Peter agreed to sell his mother's house for £495,000. The house needed a lot of work and Peter was glad to be rid of it. The survey, however, revealed an additional problem. This was a country property and the water supply and sanitation were in poor condition. The cost of works was £30,000 shared between four other properties. Quite reasonably, Peter offered to reduce the price by £6,000 to meet the buyer's share of the costs. So far so good; but when the other residents refused to believe there was a problem – pleaded poverty and so forth – the buyer pulled out. Given the costs of not doing a deal, Peter would have been well advised to have offered the buyer a £30,000 reduction on the purchase price to complete the transaction, particularly as every subsequent prospective purchaser will probably raise the same problem. Meanwhile, the house is left exposed to rain and wind.

Geetika was a wiser negotiator. When her premises burned down, the insurance company made an offer. Geetika's lawyer advised that she would probably get more if she went to court. Geetika declined to sue, however. An immediate settlement would enable her to restart in business, whereas if she went to court she would probably have to wait months for the case to come to trial, with no guarantee of success and a possible liability for costs if she lost. Likewise, a construction company had almost completed a £100 million contract when the union threatened strike action. The chief executive decided that this was no time to start exploring issues, inventing options and so forth. He confined himself to two vital questions:

1. How much do they want?
2. If I agree, will it get the job finished?

LANDING THE FISH

You not only have to hook the fish, you have to land it. Make sure you really do have an agreement that both parties understand and are ready to commit to. Failure to pin down the details can result in the fish swimming away after all, or will sow the seeds of subsequent discord. Be clear about what you are selling or buying – what exactly does the transaction include? For instance, does the sale include the customer list or just buildings and hardware? Have you checked the precise model number?

Be careful not to create unwanted legal obligations by your actions. Kaleen and Hassid were friends. They often talked about starting a business together. Kaleen eventually founded a business importing rugs. Since Hassid contributed some of the cash, Kaleen put Hassid's name on the firm's notepaper. The business failed. Creditors then sued both Kaleen and Hassid as partners. Hassid denied that he was a partner. He said he had merely put money into the business to help Kaleen. The misunderstanding arose partly because neither party realized that in English law a partnership merely comprises two or more people trading together with a view to profit. A partnership can therefore be created without express intent – a vital point, since partners are liable for the debts of the firm even though they did not incur them personally or even know about them.

TRUST

'In God we trust,' reads the notice hanging over the public bar; 'all others pay cash.' Trust means betting that another party will not take advantage of your vulnerability. Trusting someone is therefore a risky decision. Many entrepreneurs will say, 'Never trust anyone.' It is a sad but solid maxim often born of bitter experience.

Khan imported cloth into the United Kingdom. He remitted almost all of his earnings to support his family in Pakistan. He also owned a small petrol station in Pakistan managed by his brother, who also managed the family finances. One day, on a visit to Pakistan, Khan was having lunch with his brother. Khan mentioned 'his' house and 'his' petrol station. The brother interjected, 'Say again?'

'Well, it's my house, it's my land,' said Khan.

'Brother, here is nothing yours. It's all mine – nothing yours. Don't you ever say that! It's not yours: mine.'

The unfortunate Khan died shortly after this episode, his death hastened, so friends believe, by his brother's treachery.

Get it in writing.

The more important transactions should be committed to paper. Paper is extremely important because it is the means by which property rights are legally evidenced and proven. Liz and Jane owned a boarding house. They agreed that if either wanted to leave the business they would give the other party six months' notice and a year to find the money to buy them out. They had known one another for years and prided themselves on having nothing in writing. That's fine until relationships break down, or if one (or both) of the parties suddenly dies and heartbroken relatives descend like vultures on the spoils. With nothing in writing they can make all sorts of claims that are expensive, stressful and risky to defend.

Where possible, make agreements independent of trust. For example, rather than trust a prospective tenant to keep the premises in good order and pay the rent regularly, insist upon a deposit and rent in advance. Withhold part payment on contracts until all obligations are fulfilled.

Genuine trust makes money.

On a more positive note, fortunes have been built upon trust. The Quaker movement is associated with many highly successful and enduring businesses including Barclays Bank, Rowntree chocolate and Clarks shoes. Quakers prospered in business because they practised an ethic of scrupulous honesty. If a Quaker sold a pound of porridge oats or cocoa beans, the consignment weighed exactly 16 ounces. Moreover, Quakers' word was their bond. Since this was in the days before consumer protection, people were keen to deal with them.

Once the hammer falls in an auction, then in English law, unless a reserve price is imposed, both parties are bound to buy and sell at the hammer price. If the hammer price is low, sellers do not always honour their commitments, particularly in some of the more dubious car auctions. The point is that even now, surrounded though we are by reams of protective legislation, trading standards and so forth, there is no substitute for dealing with reputable firms.

Conversely, a good reputation still pays handsome dividends. Christian law firms attract business because prospective clients feel they can trust them. Reciprocal trust in business is a powerful combination. The Pullman Company (see Chapter 1) developed the ideal relationship with suppliers. Requirements were clearly specified, bills paid promptly and loyalty maintained. In return, Pullman expected to be kept supplied come what may. It was an arrangement that all parties benefited from and much more profitable in the long run than haggling over price.

Trust also promotes operational efficiency. Here is a poor and short-sighted way of doing business, as related by Rory, a greengrocer:

In the fruit business there has never been a tradition of the supplier supporting the retailer. They have always been working against each other. [For instance, in the English strawberry season] it's a product that varies from plant to plant, from field to field, so it's very difficult to get a consistent product... Out of 10 pallets of strawberries you will only get three really good ones, four average ones and three poor ones. I've seen strawberry salesmen sell the same palette of strawberries five times. So you look at a palette and you say, 'I'm having that palette, Michael, yes, that's the one, put the sticker on that palette.'

'Yes, bang! Done, Rory!'

Then when you get back to yer wagon and it's loaded up, that's not the palette you've got. And that's where the mistrust comes from because it actually goes right through it.

Both parties could save money (and aggravation) if the greengrocer could simply telephone an order, confident that the supplies would match requirements.

Here, a retail fishmonger recounts his altogether happier experience of dealing with wholesalers:

You could have gone down to the wholesale market and somebody would have sailed up to you on a Saturday – 'Oh, clear this up' (there might have been 20 stones [about 130 kilograms] of fish stuff you wouldn't want to display wholesale on a Monday) 'and just return us a price.'

And you probably would have traded on a Saturday and sold all your normal fish by about 4 o'clock and then in that last two hours, you would have sold this 20 stone – probably whatever you took out of it – you would have given him say 70 per cent or 65 per cent of what you took and the rest would have been profit.

Notice that price is a secondary concern here. The wholesaler is more interested in clearing out surplus fish (that will in any case be unsellable by Monday), hosing down the premises and getting home. Business, moreover, is done upon a basis of trust. The wholesaler relies upon the retailer to return an accurate percentage. Trust is economically efficient because it enables buyers and sellers to dispense with non-value-adding formalities such as formal written contracts. Business can proceed on the shared ethic that 'my word is my bond'.

Such relationships represent the ideal. Trust is built up over time. Meanwhile, the best advice is to make agreements independent of trust and, if possible, negotiate only with people with whom you feel comfortable.

HANDLING THE POWERFUL

What if that is not possible? It is not easy to negotiate when the other party is much more powerful. Yet appearances can be deceptive. No power relation is absolute, despite what appearances may suggest. Banks need to lend money in order to survive. Supermarkets need reliable and consistent supplies. Doctors need patients. Such dependency invariably confers some leverage and therefore room to negotiate.

That space, moreover, may be wider than you might think. Appearances reflect what the other party want you to believe. There is always another customer. Ignore the posturing and ask yourself what information the other party might be trying to conceal. For example, how many credible firms have they actually got bidding for this contract? How far short of their sales target might they be? What sort of buyers are they likely to attract? What difference could this deal make to them?

What might the other party know that you would like to know too?

Look for inconsistencies between actions and behaviour. They say they are overwhelmed with orders, so why do they keep telephoning you? If the deal is off, why are they still sitting at the table?

Invincible does not mean invulnerable.

Large organizations such as governments and supermarkets do not always play fair when negotiating with small business. They drive hard bargains and will not hesitate to cancel contracts if it suits their purpose – even though they are well aware that the result will be to ruin your business. Guy Watson, who owns an organic vegetable farm, recounts his experience of dealing with a major supermarket:

> We agreed a price... for our lettuces. A month in, they announced a six-week promotion on lettuce and wanted us to sell them at 9p each, having agreed a 14p minimum to cover the costs of production.
> ('Root Manoeuvre', *Sunday Times* Style Magazine, 31 August 2008, p 53)

Big organizations may be invincible. Even so, they are not invulnerable. Supermarkets can always find someone willing to supply cheaper chickens. Chain stores can always get someone to supply cheaper shirts. But what are the costs to the other party of not doing a deal with you? Not least is that a new supplier is an unknown quantity and therefore poses a new risk. For instance, material from different suppliers can wreak havoc with production processes even though the specifications are identical.

Incidentally, firms that push their luck by pressurizing small suppliers on price may discover that luck pushes back. The retail chain Primark discovered this to their cost. As they pushed down the price of shirts, suppliers in India simply trimmed a bit more off the tail! And the cheaper lettuce preceded the reputational damage caused by media intrusion.

ALTERNATIVES ARE POWER

Your ultimate power is to walk away. What prevents us from exercising that power is fear of the unknown. You can rid yourself of this fear by deciding in advance what you will do if you are unable to achieve a satisfactory settlement. What is the next best thing?

In other words, the purpose of generating alternatives is to protect yourself from a bad bargain by mitigating the cost of not doing a deal.

Henry owns a family-run hotel in Austria. The collapse of communism has opened up new markets, particularly from former East Germany. The trouble is, travel agents pay small hotels a pittance. Moreover, East German tourists tend to be on tight budgets. Consequently, all in all, the business involves a lot of work for meagre returns. After failing to negotiate a larger slice of the revenues from the travel agents, Henry tried something new. Rather than try to compensate for the shortfall by taking more and more unremunerative tourists, Henry built an annexe to host small conferences. The strategy worked, enabling Henry to achieve block bookings at good room rates plus conference fees. Some days he is up until 4 am serving drinks in the bar. He doesn't mind; cash tills ringing from liberal expense accounts are music to his ears!

Alternatives are always available but they may not be immediately obvious. You have to look for them and then work at them. Clare owned a bookstore. When supermarkets and large chains began undercutting prices and threatening her livelihood, Clare organized a consortium of small bookshops, placing joint orders to increase their buying power. The consortium then extended the idea to block purchases of electricity and common personnel and accountancy services.

Seek and you will find.

For all we know, Clare's initiative may become the cornerstone of a new retail empire. Business history contains many examples of the weak successfully challenging the strong, such as the Co-operative movement, CAMRA (the Campaign for Real Ale) and, more recently, Fairtrade and UK farmers' markets. At the heart of all of these initiatives is the realization that nothing need be inevitable.

YOU, THE POWERFUL

Finally, let's consider the future. When you become powerful and successful, how will you conduct yourself when negotiating with small businesses and fledgling entrepreneurs? Will you be the sort who argues with a struggling shopkeeper over 60p, who delays paying bills for good work, who haggles with a desperately poor stallholder in a market in Somalia just for the sake of it? Will yours be a destructive or a constructive contribution to the business community?

Conducted honourably, negotiations are a prime opportunity to establish relationships based upon trust and mutual acknowledgement of one another's needs — relations that can last a lifetime and create mutual prosperity. Moreover, the manner in which you conduct yourself will have a powerful impact upon parties who may not always be weak and needy. How do you want them to remember you?

Summary

1. Never negotiate over positions. Focus upon interests.

2. Price is seldom the only factor in negotiations.

3. Interests may conflict but there are frequently identical and/or mutually compatible interests as well.

4. Search for options that meet all parties' interests.

5. Try to put yourself in the other party's shoes.

6. Base discussions around market rates or some other defensible criterion.

7. Don't try to argue the other party into submission; listen and ask questions.

8. Be prepared to ask for what you want.

9. Never say 'no' when you can say 'maybe'.

10. Never negotiate when you and/or the other party feel angry.

11. Be patient.

12. Be pragmatic if the cost of not doing a deal is high.

13. Be clear about what you are agreeing to.

14. Commit important agreements to writing.

15. Reciprocal trust is economically efficient.

16. Alternatives are power.

EPILOGUE

A young entrepreneur sat down to supper with his wife. They consumed their modest meal sitting on packing crates. The young entrepreneur passed a bowl of peanuts to his wife. 'Wish they were emeralds,' he said.

Many years later they were dining in a beautiful room, sitting on antique furniture surrounded by paintings, silver and objets d'art. This time the entrepreneur pushed a bowl of emeralds towards his wife, saying, 'Wish they were peanuts.'

Moral: enjoy the journey.

Good luck!

The *Business Enterprise* series

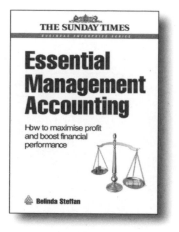